FREEZE FRESH

T0062612

FREEZE FRESH

❄

The Ultimate Guide to
PRESERVING 55 FRUITS AND VEGETABLES
for Maximum Flavor and Versatility

CRYSTAL SCHMIDT

Foreword by Eve Kilcher

Storey Publishing

The mission of Storey Publishing is to serve our customers by publishing practical information that encourages personal independence in harmony with the environment.

EDITED BY Sarah Guare Slattery and Carleen Madigan

ART DIRECTION AND BOOK DESIGN BY Carolyn Eckert

TEXT PRODUCTION BY Jennifer Jepson Smith

INDEXED BY Christine R. Lindemer, Boston Road Communications

COVER PHOTOGRAPHY BY © Robert Olding/Studio Eight

INTERIOR PHOTOGRAPHY BY © Robert Olding/Studio Eight, i–x, 2, 4, 5, 6 t., 10–15, 18–21, 30–34, 36–39, 46–48, 52, 53, 55, 59, 65, 69, 72, 73, 74 b., 75, 76 t., 80, 81, 84, 88, 91, 94, 98, 99 l., 100, 101, 103, 105, 106, 109–111, 114, 117, 118 t., 120–122, 126, 127, 130, 134, 138, 143, 145, 149, 151, 155, 160, 162, 167, 170, 173, 182, 188; © Crystal Schmidt, 1, 8, 9, 16, 17, 22, 23 m., 24, 28, 29, 35, 40–45, 49, 51, 54, 56, 57, 60–64, 66–68, 71, 74 t., 76 b., 77, 79, 83, 86, 87, 89, 92, 95–97, 99 r., 102, 104, 107, 108, 113, 115, 116, 118 b., 119, 123–125, 128, 131–133, 135, 137, 140–142, 144, 146, 148, 150, 152–154, 156, 157, 159, 161, 164–166, 168, 169, 171, 172, 174–181, 183, 185–187, 189–192

ADDITIONAL PHOTOGRAPHY BY Andrea Niosi/Unsplash, 23 t.; Courtesy of the Duane Dahnert Family, 6 b.; © Gyro/iStock.com, 23 b.; © Hector/Alamy Stock Photo, 7

FOOD STYLING BY Madeline Fitzgerald

TEXT © 2022 BY Crystal Schmidt

All rights reserved. No part of this book may be reproduced without written permission from the publisher, except by a reviewer who may quote brief passages or reproduce illustrations in a review with appropriate credits; nor may any part of this book be reproduced, stored in a retrieval system, or transmitted in any form or by any means—electronic, mechanical, photocopying, recording, or other—without written permission from the publisher.

The information in this book is true and complete to the best of our knowledge. All recommendations are made without guarantee on the part of the author or Storey Publishing. The author and publisher disclaim any liability in connection with the use of this information.

Storey books are available at special discounts when purchased in bulk for premiums and sales promotions as well as for fund-raising or educational use. Special editions or book excerpts can also be created to specification. For details, please call 800-827-8673, or send an email to sales@storey.com.

Storey Publishing
210 MASS MoCA Way
North Adams, MA 01247
storey.com

Printed in China by R.R. Donnelley

10 9 8 7 6 5 4

Library of Congress Cataloging-in-Publication Data on file

To all of the home preservers who have come before me,
who have been growing and putting up food for their
families for generations—even before the modern marvel
of refrigeration—thank you for your inspiration.

CONTENTS

FREEZING PRODUCE FROM A to Z 37

FOREWORD

BY EVE KILCHER, author of *Homestead Kitchen* and costar of *Alaska: The Last Frontier*

Growing up on a small family farm in Alaska, gardening and preserving food have been part of my life since childhood. In my twenties, I became inspired to integrate regenerative agriculture and a more self-sufficient lifestyle into my work and started a commercial organic vegetable garden on my family's property. A few years into this endeavor, the Discovery Channel contacted my husband, Eivin, and me to be part of a show they wanted to create about living off the land in Alaska, called *Alaska: The Last Frontier*. One of the greatest gifts the show has brought to my life is the ability to share with a wider audience our passion for living a healthier, more self-sufficient lifestyle in which we give back to the earth and humanity more than we take (not a small feat). I have always believed that it is important to feel connected to where our food comes from. When we do, I believe our own health and the wellbeing of our community are positively impacted. You could say that food and health are my faith and devotion.

Crystal has been such an inspiration to me, prompting me to try many new things. She truly embodies the homesteading spirit and is always willing to share her knowledge in a way that's easy to understand and approachable. Her love of heirloom beans is contagious and is what sparked our social media friendship. I am now obsessed with growing her beans in Alaska, which, let me tell you, is not easy in our short growing season! It is so neat to trade resources across the country with another food lover and gardener.

As one of the most thorough people I know and an incredible cook, Crystal is the perfect person to write a preserving and recipe book. I trust that if I follow her instructions on how to make anything, it will be successful and taste heavenly. There are few comprehensive resources for preserving food through freezing, and this book fills a huge gap. Freezing is an essential way to preserve food and is much easier and more foolproof than canning. I think the more accessible we can make food processing and home preserving, the better.

The techniques in this book will allow anyone to put up high-quality in-season produce, whether they grow it themselves or buy it in the store, to enjoy year-round. I hope you glean as much inspiration and practical knowledge from this lovely book as I have.

Welcome

❄ Whether you grow your own food, buy from a local farmer, or are simply looking to put up bulk produce that you got a good deal on, freezing is an excellent way to preserve what's in abundance now and to tuck it away for later.

All my life I've had a spark in me to grow and preserve food. One of my earliest gardening memories is of sitting in the dirt in my grandma's garden when I was just a little girl, unwrapping and eating ground cherries while she weeded. She taught my dad to garden, and he taught me. I grew up eating a lot of homegrown food, and I'm incredibly thankful for that.

There's a grocery store just 10 minutes from my house, but that doesn't stop me from putting my heart and soul into growing my own food every year. My fella, Karl, and I pack a lot of gardening into a short growing season on our homestead in Wisconsin. We preserve all we can, then ride out the winter.

For me, growing food is grounding; it makes me feel connected and whole. I share a lot of our life on social media and on my website, and I find great joy in inspiring others with what we're growing, eating, and preserving. I wish that more people could experience growing their own food. I truly think it could change the world.

Crystal

A Fresh Look at Freezing Food

In the chapters to come, you'll find three main types of content:

1 thoughtful, detailed freezing techniques for common fruits and vegetables

2 delicious recipes that freeze well, letting your produce shine

3 recipes that use frozen produce

With freezing, it's important to manage your expectations. Frozen food is tasty in its own right, but it's not the same as fresh. Freezing is an exceptional preservation tool, but most fruits and vegetables will change in the freezer, and it's helpful to recognize this. What we *can* do is be smart about what we freeze and learn to use frozen food in ways that highlight its best qualities.

There is so much joy in taking fresh produce, transforming it into delicious food that your family enjoys, and squirrelling it away.
I hope that the ideas in this book are a jumping-off point that inspires you to try freezing food in new ways.

FREEZING BASICS

❄

Why Freeze Produce?

Over the years, freezing has become my favorite way to preserve food. I still ferment, can, and dehydrate some of our homegrown produce, but the majority gets frozen. I find that freezing has some advantages over other preserving techniques, and when done properly, freezing preserves many of the valuable nutrients in fruits and vegetables.

I value the freedom that comes with freezing instead of canning. While I still follow general food-safety recommendations, it's refreshing not to have to worry about safe-canning rules, acidity, and botulism; this allows me to be more creative in the kitchen. It's almost always less work to freeze food than to can it—no standing in front of a hot canner for hours! Dehydrating can be useful, but rehydrated food, especially vegetables, always falls a little flat for me.

Freezing is a convenient way to tuck away small quantities of produce as well as items that aren't well suited for other preservation methods. A couple of pounds of tomatoes isn't enough to make canning worthwhile, but it is enough to chop up and toss in the freezer.

Early Cooling Devices

Freezing food may seem like a modern invention, but cultures have been preserving this way for ages. For as long as humans have been around, we've been preserving food—it's a basic form of survival. If you didn't grow or forage it, and if you didn't preserve it, you didn't eat. Today's preserving tools may differ from those 50, 100, or even 10,000 years ago, but the sentiment and science behind old and new methods are very much the same.

When Karl's grandpa was a young boy growing up on a rural Wisconsin farm in the 1930s, his family didn't have electric refrigeration, so they would fill an icehouse every year. In February, when the lake

Karl's grandpa as a young man, cutting blocks of ice from the frozen lake to fill the icehouse. The blocks would provide refrigeration for the warm summer months.

was deeply frozen, they would use a handheld saw to cut out 18-inch cubes of ice. It took two men to pull an ice block out of the lake and a horse to haul it up the bank. The blocks were loaded onto a bobsled and brought to the icehouse, where they were packed tightly into a 10-foot cube. After about 3 days of work the icehouse would be full, and 2 feet of dry sawdust was packed all around the ice for insulation. Because of its mass, this ice would last all summer long. The family would chip off pieces of ice and place them in the top compartment of a wooden icebox they kept on the porch. Perishable foods (mainly fresh dairy) were stored in the cabinet below. Oh, how life was different back then!

While I've always been drawn to simpler times, I do appreciate our modern technology. Indoor plumbing—inspired! Unlimited information at the click of a button—amazing! Electric refrigeration—glorious!

We sure have come a long way. There were many talented inventors who worked on developing and improving cooling technology in the late 1800s and early 1900s. Frozen food didn't have a great reputation at the time because it could only be frozen slowly, which caused it to become mushy, pale, and flavorless once thawed. In addition, those early freezers were dangerous because of the chemicals used in the cooling elements.

Frozen food as we know it today got its start in 1927, when Clarence Birdseye patented the multiplate freezing machine. This would become the precursor to modern freezing technology. This machine was able to freeze food quickly, thus preserving its quality. While working as a fur trader in northern Canada, Birdseye had observed the Inuit using ice, wind, and temperature to instantly freeze freshly caught fish. Once thawed, the fish were just as good as fresh, which he theorized was due to the speed at which

they were frozen. He wondered if this flash-freezing method could be applied to other foods as well.

In 1930, the Birds Eye Frosted Food Company launched its first line of frozen foods, advertising their June peas "as gloriously green as any you will see next summer." (Golly, don't you just love that slogan?!)

During World War II, canned goods were shipped overseas for the troops, and Americans were encouraged to buy frozen foods. The first home freezers appeared during the 1940s, but they did not go into mass production until after World War II. Here we are, nearly a century later, and I have three freezers in my home, which are my most important preserving tools!

In 1930, the Birds Eye Frosted Food Company began advertising frozen foods, like these green peas.

Blanching vegetables before freezing helps retain their quality.

The Science of Freezing Fruits & Vegetables

To freeze food properly, you don't need to understand all the scientific details of how things freeze and the consequences of that process, but there are a few principles that are worth knowing. First, when fruits and vegetables are frozen, the water in their cells turns to ice, expanding and rupturing the cell walls and releasing the liquid inside once they are thawed. This is why frozen foods typically become softer when thawed.

Second, because fruits and veggies are largely made of water, how quickly they freeze becomes important. In the *Handbook of Frozen Food Processing and Packaging*, editor Da-Wen Sun explains that when water freezes, ice crystals are formed first, and then they increase in size. How large the ice crystals become is determined by the rate at which the object is frozen. Fast freezing will create a larger quantity of small crystals, which are less likely to rupture the cells. Slow freezing creates big crystals that rupture a lot of cell walls and leave your produce mushy once thawed. Freezing fast = good.

Here are some things you can do to encourage rapid freezing.

- Use a dedicated freezer set to 0°F (−18°C) instead of the freezer attached to your refrigerator, which isn't quite as cold.

- Make sure that produce is cooled before putting it in the freezer. Many cooked foods can be prechilled overnight in the refrigerator before freezing.

- Don't overload the freezer by filling it with too many unfrozen items all at once. If freezing a large quantity of items, spread them out inside the freezer instead of piling them on or near each other.

HOW LONG DOES FROZEN FOOD LAST?

Under ideal conditions, cooked or blanched vegetables will keep for 1 year, and vegetables that were frozen raw will keep for 6 months. The extra longevity is why I almost always blanch my vegetables before freezing. Fruits will easily last a year.

Food kept frozen below 0°F (−18°C) will be safe to eat indefinitely. The question of "how long food lasts" is only a matter of quality, and it depends on factors such as the condition of the food when it was frozen, how it was prepared, what type of container it was frozen in, and the temperature of the freezer.

I try to freeze enough produce to last 1 year's time plus a little extra. Nutrients will slowly degrade over time, even when perfect freezing conditions are met, so keeping produce for more than a year isn't ideal.

Essential Freezing Techniques

Successful freezing is all in the details! While freezing is certainly not difficult, mastering these techniques will ensure that your frozen produce turns out exceptional. Everything from choosing the right type of freezer container to selecting the right blanching method and even thawing your food properly will impact its quality.

WASHING

If the produce is dirty, wash and scrub it until clean *before* freezing. If the produce is not obviously dirty, it's up to you whether or not to wash it.

All produce should go into the freezer as dry as possible. Because fruit won't be blanched, washing and drying it is a time-consuming extra step. If we grew the fruit ourselves and picked it with clean hands into clean buckets, I don't wash it unless it has visible dirt. If the vegetables will be blanched, I typically give them a quick rinse first, as rinsing doesn't take much time and they're going to get wet anyway.

BLANCHING

All fruits and vegetables contain enzymes that cause them to deteriorate over time. Freezing slows this enzymatic activity but does not stop it completely. The higher acidity of fruit naturally neutralizes the enzymes, but most vegetables need to be heated briefly (blanched) to deactivate these enzymes. Blanching is typically done by quickly steaming vegetables or submerging them in boiling water, then cooling them rapidly to stop the cooking. Not only will blanched vegetables have better color and flavor, but they also retain more nutrients over time than raw.

There is no one-size-fits-all blanching protocol. Each vegetable should be treated differently based on its individual characteristics—some do better with steam, for instance, and some with boiling water. In this book, blanching methods and times, as well as whether or not to use an ice bath, are listed for each vegetable and are based on the vegetable's size, density, and amount of exposed surface area.

Trim and cut veggies before blanching. For example, green bean stems should be snapped off and broccoli should be broken into florets.

FOOD QUALITY MATTERS

Only freeze the highest-quality fruits and vegetables. If something's mushy, rotten, or moldy, it isn't going to improve in the freezer. Rule of thumb: If you wouldn't eat it fresh, don't freeze it.

Produce starts to lose nutrients soon after it is picked, so get processing as quickly as possible while produce is at its peak! While freezing is sometimes a last-ditch effort (ever throw brown bananas into the freezer?), I try to freeze produce before it starts going downhill if I know we won't be able to eat it in time.

STEAM BLANCHING

1 **Prepare the steamer.** Place a steamer insert in a pot, then fill with enough water to cover the bottom of the pot but not so much that the water touches the steamer insert. A pot that comes with a fitted steamer insert works best, but you can also use a steamer basket that sits loosely in the pot. Cover the pot and bring the water to a boil over medium heat.

2 **Prepare an ice bath, if indicated.** Fill a large bowl with approximately equal parts ice and water. If you don't have ice readily available, you can use very cold tap water, although it will need to be replaced between each batch. Vegetables that are chopped into small pieces or are prone to becoming waterlogged may not need an ice bath.

3 **Add the vegetables to the steamer.** When the pot is filled with steam, place the prepared vegetables into the steamer insert. Don't overcrowd the pot—about half full is a good amount. Replace the lid.

4 **Start the timer.** Because the pot will already be up to temperature, start a timer immediately. Steam the vegetables for the time indicated, using tongs to toss the vegetables at the half-way point so they cook evenly. When working through a large quantity of vegetables, make sure to periodically check the water level. Letting your steamer pot run dry can ruin it.

5 **Place the blanched vegetables in the ice bath, if using.** Once the vegetables are blanched, immediately transfer them to the ice bath to stop the cooking. Add more ice between batches to ensure the ice bath stays very cold.

6   **Dry the vegetables.** Line a large baking pan with towels. Lift the cool vegetables from the ice bath and place them in a colander or mesh sieve to drip-dry for a few seconds, then spread the vegetables on the prepared pan. Allow the vegetables to sit until they are reasonably dry, 30 to 60 minutes, before packing them into freezer containers. If working through a lot of veggies, use multiple pans and consider turning on a small countertop fan to speed drying.

BOILING-WATER BLANCHING

1 **Prepare the pot.** Bring a large pot of water to a rolling boil.

2 **Prepare an ice bath, if indicated.** Fill a large bowl with approximately equal parts ice and water. If you don't have ice readily available, you can use very cold tap water, although it will need to be replaced between each batch. Vegetables that are chopped into small pieces or are prone to becoming waterlogged may not need an ice bath.

3 **Add the vegetables.** Place the prepared vegetables in the boiling water, being careful not to overcrowd the pot. If it takes more than 1 minute for the water to return to a boil after the vegetables are added, you've put in too much; add less in the next batch.

4 **Start the timer.** After the water returns to a boil, start the timer and cook for the time indicated. It's important to hit the time exactly and not go over or under.

5 **Place the blanched vegetables in the ice bath, if using.** Once the vegetables are blanched, immediately transfer them to the ice bath to stop the cooking. Add more ice between batches to ensure the ice bath stays very cold.

6 **Dry the vegetables.** Line a large baking pan with towels. Lift the cool vegetables from the ice bath and place them in a colander or mesh sieve to drip-dry for a few seconds, then spread the vegetables on the prepared pan. Allow the vegetables to sit until they are reasonably dry, 30 to 60 minutes, before packing them into freezer containers. If working through a lot of veggies, use multiple pans and consider turning on a small countertop fan to speed drying.

Flash freezing, or freezing food in individual pieces, can be handy for making smoothies.

FLASH FREEZING

For the home preserver, "flash freezing" is the technique of freezing individual pieces of food separately, rather than packing fresh food together in a container and then freezing it. Because there is space around each item, cold air can circulate directly around the food, which causes it to freeze quickly. Flash frozen food won't be stuck together in a clump, making it easier to use in small quantities.

Most store-bought frozen vegetables are flash frozen, which is why they are loose in the bag. With home freezing, this isn't always practical. Vegetables cut into small pieces (such as shredded carrots or cauliflower rice) would be difficult to flash freeze. Large items (such as broccoli florets or French fries) might require many pans to flash freeze, and it may be difficult to find room for all of them in the freezer.

I like to flash freeze fruits meant for smoothies, but fruits meant for baking are frozen together in a bag. Some fruits (such as blueberries) aren't prone to sticking together and therefore don't require flash freezing.

HOW TO FLASH FREEZE

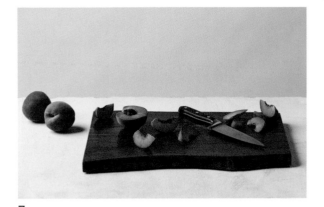

1 **Prep the produce.** Follow the prep instructions for each fruit or vegetable, including blanching, cooling, and drying, if indicated.

2 **Line a pan with parchment paper.** Place the produce on the prepared pan in a single layer with none of the pieces touching. The parchment will prevent the food from sticking to the pan.

3 **Add a double layer, if desired.** Most fruits and vegetables can be flash frozen in a double layer, which is helpful if you don't have enough room in the freezer for multiple pans. Place a piece of parchment paper over the first layer of produce, then add a second layer of produce on top of it.

4 **Place the entire pan in the freezer.** Leave it there until the produce is completely frozen. I will often leave the pan in the freezer overnight.

5 **Pack the produce.** Remove the produce from the pan and pack it into freezer containers for storage. In most cases, flash-frozen foods will pack best in freezer bags. Because the produce will be loose in the bag, it can be frozen in multiple small bags (such as quart) or fewer large bags (such as gallon).

When thawing food in the refrigerator, place the containers on a tray to catch condensation and leaks.

THAWING

According to the USDA, there are three safe ways to thaw frozen foods:

1. in the refrigerator overnight
2. in cold water
3. in the microwave

Although I won't say I've never done it before, it is considered unsafe to leave food out at room temperature to thaw. Once food reaches 40°F (4°C) or warmer, any bacteria present will begin to multiply. While food that is thawing at room temperature may still have a frozen center, the outer layer can easily enter into the "danger zone" of food safety, which is between 40°F and 140°F (4°C and 60°C). This is when bacteria can multiply rapidly.

A good rule of thumb to follow is that if the food will be heated or cooked, it's okay to thaw it using heat, like the microwave. If the food will be served or used raw, thaw it in the refrigerator or with cold water and avoid heating it.

Thawing Overnight in the Refrigerator

This is my preferred method for thawing most things, but it does require planning ahead. Smaller rigid containers and quart freezer bags will usually thaw overnight, but larger rigid containers and gallon freezer bags may take up to 2 days.

I always place thawing food containers on a pan to catch condensation and to prevent puddles in the refrigerator. This is also a smart food safety precaution in case the container leaks.

Thawing in the refrigerator is the only safe way to thaw food that was frozen in glass. Never thaw glass containers in cold water or in the microwave.

Thawing in Cold Water

To thaw in cold water, fill a bowl with very cold tap water and submerge the container in the bowl. Change the water every 30 minutes to ensure that it stays cold, and use the food immediately after thawing.

Submerge freezer containers in cold water to thaw them quickly without the use of heat.

Freezer burn is easily prevented by following a few simple guidelines.

Thawing in the Microwave

Most microwaves have a half-power or defrost setting, which warms gently and does a better job of thawing food without cooking it. Food thawed in the microwave may become slightly heated, so be prepared to use it immediately. This is always my last choice for thawing, and I use this technique only if I'm in a hurry.

PREVENTING FREEZER BURN

Freezer burn happens when food is damaged by dehydration and oxidation. Freezer burn isn't a matter of food safety (it will not make you sick) but of food quality. Freezer-burned food does not taste good. Removing the freezer-burned parts may make the remaining food salvageable, but there's a chance it still won't taste quite right, so consume with caution. Here's how to prevent freezer burn.

- **Use proper packaging.** Poor packaging is a common cause of freezer burn. Use the correct size and type of container and make sure to remove as much air as possible.

- **Keep the freezer cold.** Food can become burned if the freezer isn't cold enough. A well-sealing freezer set below 0°F (–18°C) is ideal.

- **Don't linger!** Decide what you will take out of the freezer before you open the door, grab the item quickly, and shut the door. Keep that cold air in!

- **Rotate your inventory.** The longer an item stays in the freezer, the more likely it is to develop freezer burn. Maintain an accurate inventory, making sure to eat the oldest items first.

SHOULD YOU REFREEZE PRODUCE?

According to the USDA, raw or cooked produce can be refrozen safely as long as it has been kept below 40°F (4°C). It is not safe to refreeze produce that has been left outside the refrigerator for more than 2 hours.

While it is safe to refreeze produce, this should generally be avoided because the quality of the produce can suffer greatly, depending on what it is. When you refreeze a small component of a dish, such as herbs in a casserole or onions in a soup, you are less likely to notice a reduction in quality than if you refreeze a package of green beans and then eat them on their own.

Freeze produce in bags that are meant for the freezer, which are made of thick plastic or silicone.

Types of Freezer Containers

Your choice of freezer container can make or break your frozen produce, and selecting the best container for what you're freezing will make all the difference in how long your goods will keep. The size and material of your freezer containers impact the quality and taste of food once thawed.

PLASTIC FREEZER BAGS

Bags excel at holding food that is bulky or large, like green beans and apple slices. I don't use bags for thicker sauces, such as apple butter or pesto, because those foods tend to stick inside the bag and are difficult to remove.

Freezer bags are made of thick plastic that protects food; bags labeled for "storage" are much thinner. There is some variation in thickness of freezer bags between brands. I prefer Ziploc. They cost a little more than generic, but it's worth it to me for the extra

reliability. I prefer a zip top over a slider top because it's easier to remove the air from and to seal zip-top bags.

RIGID PLASTIC CONTAINERS

Rigid containers are great for things that will go from the freezer into the fridge and may be used frequently, such as jam or pickles. I also prefer rigid containers for thick sauces and anything frozen in smaller quantities. Rigid containers are not well suited for food that is bulky, such as broccoli florets or zucchini pieces, because it's hard to remove the air between the pieces.

Rigid containers are typically reusable and also do a good job of protecting food. Just make sure to select products that are intended for freezer use. My favorite are Reditainer Extreme Freeze containers, which I order online. They are reusable for years, are inexpensive, and come in a variety of sizes. While you can use recycled containers from things like

If freezing in glass, make sure to choose containers that have straight sides.

restaurant takeout and yogurt, they aren't as thick and they tend to crack easily in the freezer.

GLASS CONTAINERS

Whether or not to freeze in glass can be a hot topic among preservers. Glass is a clean and green choice because it is reusable and doesn't contain harmful chemicals. Glass containers also do a good job of protecting food. The downside is that breakage is almost inevitable from time to time. It's not safe to eat the contents of a cracked jar because there could be small shards of glass in it, so the food must be thrown out.

Here are tips for freezing in glass and minimizing breakage.

- **Only use straight-sided jars.** Most widemouthed canning jars and cylindrical Weck brand jars are suitable for freezing, but jars with "shoulders," such as regular pint or quart jars, have a much higher risk of breaking. Always check with the manufacturer to make sure your glass is rated for freezing.

- **Leave plenty of headspace.** Food will expand when it is frozen, so leave ample room between the food and the top of the jar to prevent breakage, about 2 inches in a quart jar and slightly less for smaller jars.

- **Always prechill food in the refrigerator.** This is especially important for liquids. Putting warm food into a jar and placing that jar straight into the freezer will almost guarantee a crack.

- **Make sure glass jars can stand upright in the freezer.** Food expands outward in addition to upward as it freezes. This slight pressure on the walls of the jar, combined with it bumping against another jar, may cause it to crack. Because of this, an upright freezer with shelves is a better choice than a chest freezer if you intend to freeze in glass.

Silicone is a great choice for molds because the food is easy to remove and the silicone doesn't hold on to odors. Plastic and metal molds also work well.

VACUUM-SEALED BAGS

Vacuum sealing removes nearly all the air in the bag, which means food will last longer and be less prone to freezer burn. While this is a good option, we home preservers can still achieve great results without this expensive, specialized piece of equipment.

SILICONE FREEZER CONTAINERS

Reusable bags made from silicone can be used in the freezer and do a good job of protecting food. The downsides are that it's difficult to remove air from these bags and they are wildly expensive compared to other options.

FREEZER & BUTCHER PAPER

Produce contains a lot of moisture and does best when frozen in something watertight. Freezer paper or butcher paper isn't a good option for most fruits and vegetables.

MOLDS

Molds, such as silicone muffin pans and plastic ice cube trays, can be useful for freezing smaller quantities. There are many different sizes and shapes of molds available, but the two sizes I use the most are ice cube size (about 2 tablespoons) and standard muffin size (about ½ cup). My favorite brand of silicone molds is Souper Cubes. They come in multiple sizes, and the frozen blocks fit perfectly in standard freezer bags.

I prefer good-quality silicone molds because they don't stain or hold odors, and the frozen items pop right out. Plastic ice cube trays are cheap and most people already have them, but odors from strongly flavored foods are hard to get out.

To freeze in molds, follow the prep instructions for each type of produce—including blanching, cooling, and drying, if indicated. Fill the mold and place it in the freezer until completely frozen. Pop the produce out of the mold and pack it into containers. Freezer bags usually work best for foods frozen in molds.

REMOVING AIR FROM CONTAINERS

Air is the enemy of frozen food, so it's important to remove as much of it as possible before sealing the freezer container. Exposure to oxygen will cause freezer burn and lower the quality of frozen food over time.

If you are using rigid containers, the only way to remove air is with a vacuum sealer, so it's important to choose the right size container. Make sure to fill the container almost to the top, leaving just enough headspace for the food to expand. There is no space for air to linger in a full container, but plenty of room in one that is only half full.

If you are using freezer bags, remove as much air as reasonably possible but don't fuss over getting it perfect. Here is my preferred method.

1   Gently flatten the produce in the bag so that it is a uniform thickness.

2   Close the seal except for the very corner.

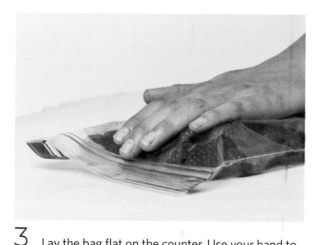

3   Lay the bag flat on the counter. Use your hand to press down on it, expelling the air inside.

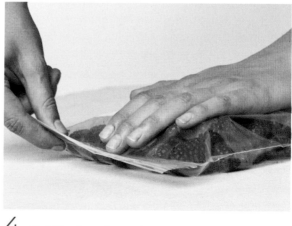

4   Quickly close the seal.

Use good-quality, name-brand tape and a permanent marker to label reusable freezer containers.

Labeling Containers

It is important to label what you're putting into the freezer. You may think you'll remember ("I'll use all of this before next season!"), or that the contents will be obvious ("Clearly this is a bag of cherry tomatoes!"), but I promise that you'll never regret labeling your goods.

What to include on the label. At the very least, place the year on the label so that you (or someone else) will know which containers should be used first. For produce that we harvest and freeze multiple times during the season, such as green beans and berries, I include the month as well as the year. That way, if there were a question of safety or quality (although such situations are rare), I could identify the bags harvested around the same time. A brief description of the contents is nice too.

For things that I often use in baking or cooking, such as shredded zucchini or pumpkin purée, I measure the quantity before freezing and mark it on the container. If you know how much of an ingredient your favorite recipes call for, it's very handy to freeze exactly that amount.

What to use for labeling. It's quick and effective to write directly on freezer bags using a permanent marker. The ink won't rub off if you write in the designated labeling area printed on most bags. I keep a marker inside my kitchen utensil drawer so it's always handy.

Reusable containers should be labeled with a piece of tape that can be removed, so the containers can be used and relabeled. Beware: Some tapes stick better than others, and it's a real pain when your labels fall off. I recommend the following:

- **Freezer tape.** It is made to stick in cold temperatures, although it can be more expensive and harder to find.
- **High-quality masking tape.** I like both Scotch and Duck brands; in my experience, generic tape doesn't stick as well.
- **Green or blue painter's tape.** This holds its stick reliably in the freezer. It's also easy to source, and you may already have some lying around.

Not only do these three tapes stick well, but they are easy to remove and don't leave residue on your containers.

Helpful Tools & Supplies

I use a handful of tools and other products and supplies frequently in this book. The following are very helpful for freezing the harvest.

KITCHEN TOOLS

Blender. I rely on my blender frequently when preserving, especially for puréeing sauces. An immersion blender can also be used, but in most cases I prefer a countertop model because it's more powerful.

Fine-mesh sieve. A metal mesh sieve is useful for tasks such as removing seeds from raspberry purée and skins and seeds from tomato sauce. This simple tool is an important workhorse in my preserving kitchen.

Food processor. A food processor excels at chopping, slicing, shredding, and grating, thanks to its attachments. In most cases, a blender is a fine substitute.

Half sheet baking pans. While most recipes in this book can be adapted to whatever size baking pans you have, large 18- by 13-inch baking pans are indispensable for processing a lot of produce at once. I use these for my everyday cooking too.

Mandoline slicer. This tool slices produce quickly and in uniform slices, which is especially helpful for making things such as pickle chips.

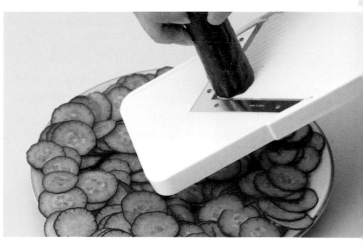

Sharp knives. Having a good, sharp knife makes all the difference when you are prepping fruits and veggies, particularly if you're working through large quantities of them. A dull knife can tear and bruise produce, which will affect its quality.

Tape measure or ruler. In several instances in this book, I ask you to cut vegetables to a specific size, and being accurate is important. Keep a small measuring tape in the kitchen for this purpose.

CONSUMABLE SUPPLIES

All-purpose and gluten-free flours. Almost all the recipes in this book that call for flour were developed and tested using organic all-purpose flour and a gluten-free flour blend. If using gluten-free flour, it's important to select a blend that is made to be used as a 1:1 substitute for all-purpose flour. My preferred brands are Pamela's Gluten-Free All-Purpose Flour and Bob's Red Mill Gluten Free 1-to-1 Baking Flour.

Butter. You'll notice that I don't specify whether to use salted or unsalted butter in the recipes. I always use salted butter, but the recipes will turn out fine with unsalted as well, so use what you prefer or already have on hand.

Extra-virgin olive oil. I use this oil in most of my cooking because it's healthy and I like the taste. Good-quality olive oil is safe to cook with at moderately high temperatures. You can substitute avocado oil or another neutral-tasting oil in its place for most of the recipes in this book.

Ice pop bags. Zip-top tubes that you can fill and close yourself are incredibly fun, and they are actually very easy to use! You can find these online and at specialty kitchen stores.

Lemon and lime juice. Citrus juice is used for flavor, and freshly squeezed lemon and lime juice is best.

Parchment paper or silicone baking mat. Parchment paper is typically coated with a thin layer of silicone, making it nonstick. It prevents food from adhering to the pan when flash freezing. A silicone baking mat is a fine substitute.

Sea salt. You'll notice that all my recipes call for sea salt. I much prefer the delicate flavor and extra dose of minerals that comes from using sea salt instead of iodized table salt or kosher salt. Salt is for taste and is not an integral part of preservation by freezing.

Sugar. While sugar is necessary in some recipes, I've indicated the places where it can be left out or a different sweetener can be substituted.

Vinegars. For the purpose of freezing, vinegar is used for taste and not to establish a safe acidity level as in canning. Quality matters, especially with distilled white vinegar—some generic vinegars can be very harsh, so I use only Heinz brand or any organic product.

All about Freezers

To produce the best-quality frozen food, I recommend using a dedicated freezer, which is made for freezing only, not refrigeration. This type of freezer is colder than the freezer attached to your refrigerator and will freeze food faster, thus producing better quality food. A refrigerator-freezer will also work for freezing food, and you'll still be able to attain good results if that's all you have.

A freezer is an investment, so it's important to buy one that will meet your needs and fit well in your space. Knowing how to properly care for a freezer will ensure that it lasts for years and keeps all your tasty goods tucked away and deeply frozen!

There are two main types of dedicated freezers: upright and chest. Both have pros and cons and important differences to consider.

UPRIGHT FREEZERS

An upright freezer has a door that opens outward like a refrigerator, and it has shelves inside.

PROS

- Most people find this type of freezer easier to load and unload and easier to keep organized because it has shelves. For anyone with physical limitations, or who has trouble bending over or lifting, an upright freezer might be a better choice.

- If you freeze in glass containers, it's helpful to be able to store the jars on shelves to prevent them from clanking together and cracking.

- An upright takes up less floor space and is more likely to be available in colors other than white.

CONS

- The shelves inside are nice for organizing, but they might not accommodate large or oddly shaped items.

- During a power outage, an upright freezer will thaw approximately 1 day faster than a chest freezer. This might be an important consideration if you live somewhere that loses power frequently.

- If your upright freezer is self-defrosting, it won't stay as consistently cold, and the fluctuating temperature can encourage freezer burn. The motor cycling on and off tends to make self-defrosting uprights noisier as well.

CHEST FREEZERS

The door is on the top of a chest freezer, and it opens upward like a treasure chest.

PROS

- It has more usable space inside compared to an upright freezer.

- It is typically less expensive to buy and more energy efficient to operate than an upright freezer.

- Because of the way everything packs snugly into a chest freezer, it has a large amount of thermal mass and food will stay frozen longer if the power goes out than it will in an upright.

- Because they have fewer components, manual-defrost chest freezers have a slightly longer life span than self-defrosting upright freezers.

CONS

- Most chest freezers are only sold in white and look very utilitarian.

- Chest freezers take up more floor space and are harder to keep organized. If you don't have a good organizational system (don't fret, I'll share mine on page 28), it can feel like a black hole where food gets lost.

- Because the freezer is so deep, some folks have difficulty reaching the bottom. I am 5 feet 6 inches tall and can place my hand on the very bottom of the freezer if I stand on my tippy toes!

- Chest freezers typically need to be defrosted manually, which isn't that bad a task. It takes Karl and me just under an hour to unload, defrost, clean, and reload our large 24-cubic-foot chest freezer. We do this once, or sometimes twice, per year.

INSTALLATION CONSIDERATIONS

It's helpful to browse through the user's manual of the specific freezer you're considering before purchasing it. These can usually be found online. Here are some practical considerations to make before purchasing a freezer.

- Freezers should not be placed in an area that gets too cold or too warm, such as an outdoor building or garage; you can find ambient temperature guidelines in the manual.

TEMPERATURE MONITORS & ALARMS

It would be devastating to lose all the food in your freezer because of a malfunction or the cord becoming unplugged. Some freezer models have an electronic display that shows the internal temperature and indicates whether the freezer has lost power and for how long. Freezers with this feature may also have an alarm that sounds if the temperature rises above a certain level or if the door is left ajar.

Our freezers don't have this feature, so we added our own. We use a SensorPush brand thermometer, which sits in the freezer and tracks the temperature. This data is viewed in a smartphone app, which also sends a notification if the freezer is getting too warm.

- When measuring to see what size freezer will fit in your space, be sure to allow for the required airspace around it. Don't forget to check if the door will have enough room to fully open out or up.

- Always place a freezer in a dry, level area. Keep the freezer in a cool space, out of direct sunlight, and away from other appliances that give off heat.

- Most manufacturers recommend that freezers be plugged directly into a grounded wall socket, which may influence where you can put your model (using a power strip or extension cord can even void the warranty). Some freezers may require a dedicated outlet.

- Most modern freezers are narrow enough to fit through standard doorways, but it's always a good idea to check the corners and turns your chosen model will need to travel through to reach its final destination.

DEFROSTING

For most freezers, defrosting is a necessary part of good maintenance. As ice builds up, it can accumulate near the door and make the door difficult to close and seal properly. This can lead to temperature fluctuations and freezer burn, and it also decreases the life span of the freezer.

We typically defrost our freezers in early summer, before we start filling them with the year's harvest. Most manufacturers recommend defrosting when the ice buildup is ¼ to ½ inch thick, although you should follow the recommendation for your particular freezer.

If your freezer needs further cleaning, always consult your manual to see which types of cleaners should or shouldn't be used.

HOW TO MANUALLY DEFROST A CHEST OR UPRIGHT FREEZER

1 **Unplug.** Most brands recommend unplugging rather than just turning off the freezer for defrosting. If you're prone to forgetting things, leave a note on the door or set a reminder on your phone to plug the freezer back in when you're done.

2 **Empty.** Remove everything from the freezer and stack it on the floor near the freezer. Cover the frozen food with several heavy blankets to insulate it while you work. If the freezer is in a location where the floor isn't clean, lay down a tarp or blanket first. Alternatively, place the frozen food in coolers.

3 **Thaw.** Position a household fan to blow air into the freezer to help push out the cold air. This is especially important to do for a chest freezer, because cold air sinks, and the lower area is slow to warm up. Let the freezer thaw until the ice buildup starts to release from the sides, 5 to 10 minutes. Wait for the ice to let go naturally—do not pry it off or use warm water or warm air. This waiting time can be a good opportunity to organize and inventory the freezer contents.

4 **Remove ice.** Gently slide the ice chunks to the bottom of the freezer, then scoop them out and into a bucket. Never use a metal scoop, as it could scratch the inside of the freezer. A plastic dustpan or a thin-walled plastic container works well for scooping. Most chest freezers will have a drain on the bottom with a plug. This can be helpful in certain situations, but we've never used it during our yearly defrosting.

5 **Dry.** Use towels to dry the inner side walls and to soak up any remaining water from the bottom. When you're finished, the freezer should be completely dry to the touch.

6 **Replug.** Plug the freezer back in—don't forget this step! Most freezers have a power indicator light on the outside or an interior lightbulb to let you know that the appliance is receiving power.

7 **Refill.** Load everything back into the freezer immediately. There is no need to wait until the freezer chills again.

SELF-DEFROSTING FREEZERS

Some freezers are "frost-free" or self-defrosting and may not need to be manually defrosted. These work by having a heating element that periodically turns on and melts any ice buildup, which then exits the freezer through a drain and evaporates.

We use cardboard boxes in our chest freezer to help us organize. They make it easier to get to the contents at the bottom.

ORGANIZING A CHEST FREEZER

An upright freezer is naturally easier to keep tidy because it has built-in shelves. You can organize food in rows or stacks on the shelves, or in labeled boxes or plastic bins. Maintaining an organized chest freezer isn't difficult, but it does take more discipline. The payoff for organization is worth it—you'll be able to easily find what you're looking for, and the freezer won't become a burden to use.

We organize our chest freezers using open-top cardboard boxes. This allows us to quickly and easily lift out the upper boxes to get to the lower ones without having to swim through a sea of loose bags and packages every time we need something from the bottom. I can't imagine maintaining a large freezer without this system!

We organize by type, meaning that like things are grouped together. There are individual boxes dedicated to fruits, vegetables, tomato products, condiments, and homemade "convenience" foods such as soup and prepared side dishes for days when we need a quick-and-easy supper. I like this approach because

it's easy to see how many of each type of item I have, and I know right where to find it. Additionally, items we use often go toward the top, and things we use less frequently go toward the bottom. Of course, you should organize your freezer in a way that works for you, but this categorization approach has proven to be a winner for us!

The size of the freezer will determine what size boxes to use. For our large chest freezers, we like banana boxes—the cartons in which bananas are shipped to the grocery store. If you ask politely, the produce manager will usually give them to you. Banana boxes are sturdy without being bulky, they have handles for easy lifting, and they fit nicely in the freezer and stack well. If they are too tall, simply cut them down to a customized size for your freezer.

Bankers boxes or copy paper boxes are good fits for smaller freezers. Shipping boxes can be used, but you might have to cut your own handles to make for easier lifting. Brown paper grocery bags or reusable shopping bags also work for organizing different categories of things, although they aren't quite as easy to move in and out of the freezer as boxes.

MAINTAINING AN ORGANIZED FREEZER

There's nothing worse than the feeling of defeat that comes from knowing you have good food in the freezer that needs to be eaten but you can't find it, or you cringe at the thought of having to dig for it. Whenever I start to feel this way, that means it's time to reorganize!

During the busy preserving season, the freezer quickly becomes disheveled because I'm adding to it nearly every day. Bags of produce are strewn about, and the freezer needs a 5-minute weekly reorganization. This is when I move recently frozen items to the bottom in order to make room near the top for more incoming goods. During the off-season, this weekly organization isn't necessary.

In fall, when the freezers are full, we do a major organization to set us off on the right foot for the season of eating ahead. This involves taking everything out, grouping like things together, and reassessing our inventory.

It's a good idea to keep and update a list of what is in your freezer. It will show you which things need to be eaten faster to use them up or slower to make them last. A freezer inventory is also a convenient resource for meal planning! A quick glance at your list will give inspiration for the week's meals and ensure that you use up all the precious goods that you so diligently worked to preserve. I prefer to keep a simple handwritten list on a clipboard next to the freezer, but you can use anything from a dry-erase board to a spreadsheet or list-making app on your smartphone. Whenever something comes out of the freezer, we mark it off the list, which takes only a few seconds. Even if you forget to make a note from time to time, having an imperfect list is better than no list at all.

Special Techniques for Freezing & Working with Frozen Foods

While much of this book focuses on preserving and using individual fruits and vegetables, the following tips apply to a wider range of produce. Use these methods to help inspire creativity in the kitchen!

FREEZING TRADITIONAL PRESERVES

I've never met a jam or jelly that didn't freeze well! And I'm not talking about "freezer jam"—the technique of mixing crushed fruit with boiling sugar water and pectin, then freezing it. Because it isn't cooked, freezer jam retains a fresh flavor. However, it often uses twice as much sugar as fruit, and for this reason, I'm not fond of it.

Almost any jam recipe, even if it's meant for canning, can be frozen instead. This is a time-saving way to preserve small batches of jam when you don't want to lug out the canner and heat up the kitchen. Instead of placing the jars in the canner, put them in the refrigerator to chill overnight, then move them to the freezer. I prefer to freeze jams, jellies, and preserves in glass jelly jars because I think the contents deserve an especially elegant container.

For jammy inspirations, check out my Strawberry Sun Freezer Jam (page 163), Roasted Peach Jam (page 128), and Fig & Honey Preserves (page 96).

Can you make jams, jellies, and preserves with frozen fruit?

Yes! Hold the fruit in the freezer until you're ready to make jam or have enough stockpiled for a large batch. Using frozen fruit will also enable you to combine ingredients harvested in different seasons and create new flavor combinations.

COMBINING VEGETABLES

Get creative with freezing your produce! Combining multiple types of vegetables together in one container is a fun way to add variety to your meals. Process each vegetable according to its specific directions and simply load them into a freezer bag together. It is best if all the vegetables are cut into similar-size pieces. If all the vegetables in a blend aren't ready for harvest at the same time, flash freeze each vegetable as it becomes available so it can be easily mixed.

Try these combinations:

- Green beans + zucchini
- Peas + carrots
- Eggplant + zucchini + bell peppers
- Cauliflower + broccoli + carrots
- Bell peppers + broccoli + carrots
- Corn + carrots + green beans + peas

FREEZING GREEN JUICE

If you have a surplus of produce, juicing it and freezing the juice is a great way to preserve it. Green juice can be thawed for drinking, or frozen juice cubes can be added directly to smoothies. Green juice is flexible and can be made from whatever fruits and veggies you have on hand. My favorite combination is:

4   celery stalks

8   parsley sprigs

½   large cucumber

2   green apples, cored

1   handful kale or spinach

Juice of 1 lemon

For a pulp-free juice, cut the ingredients into pieces that fit into the hopper of your juicer, and juice them in the order listed above. For pulpy juice that contains fiber, the ingredients can simply be blended. Because it is liquid, green juice packs best in rigid containers. Consider freezing smaller portions in an ice cube tray. Be mindful that because it is raw, green juice should be used within 6 months of freezing.

HOW TO MAKE BAKED DESSERTS USING FROZEN FRUIT

Because frozen fruit releases more liquid, it doesn't behave quite the same way as fresh in desserts where a large quantity is baked together, such as in a pie, crisp, or cobbler. Sugar and thickener don't stick well to frozen fruit and will just sink to the bottom of the dish. Thawed fruit will be watery and difficult to work with. My preferred method for using frozen fruit in these types of desserts is to cook the filling before baking. I've given some suggestions with specific measurements on page 34, but this technique can be adapted to many types and combinations of fruit and baked goods, so feel free to experiment!

1 **Heat the frozen fruit in a pot over medium heat.**
Add a small amount of lemon juice or other citrus juice (to enhance the flavor of the fruit), and stir frequently with a silicone spatula until the fruit is thawed, 10 to 15 minutes. Stir gently, so as to not break up the fruit.

2 **Combine the sugar and thickener** (usually cornstarch or flour). Mix these together in a bowl, along with the salt and any dry spices such as cinnamon. This will prevent the thickener from clumping when it's added to the hot fruit. Frozen fruit will typically give off a little more liquid than fresh, so I use slightly more thickener for frozen fruit than I would for fresh.

3 **Stir the sugar mixture into the fruit and bring to a boil.**
Cook for several minutes over medium heat, stirring continuously until the fruit thickens. Because the fruit is thickened before being baked, you can see ahead of time if the consistency is correct or if you need to add more thickener.

4 **Add any wet seasonings,** such as vanilla extract or lemon zest.

5 **Allow the filling to cool.**
Then use it in a pie, crisp, or cobbler. Putting hot filling in a piecrust will cause the crust to become soggy.

6 **Bake as directed in the recipe.**

FAVORITE PIE, COBBLER, AND CRISP FILLINGS

Blueberry

6 cups frozen blueberries

1 tablespoon lemon juice

⅔ cup sugar

¼ cup cornstarch

¼ teaspoon sea salt

1 teaspoon vanilla extract

1 teaspoon finely grated lemon zest (optional)

Peach

8 cups frozen peeled, sliced peaches

1 tablespoon lemon juice

¼ cup brown sugar

¼ cup granulated sugar

¼ cup cornstarch

½ teaspoon ground cinnamon

¼ teaspoon sea salt

1 teaspoon vanilla extract

Cherry

6 cups frozen pitted tart cherries

1 tablespoon lemon juice

⅔ cup sugar

¼ cup plus 1 tablespoon cornstarch

¼ teaspoon sea salt

½ teaspoon vanilla extract

½ teaspoon almond extract

Strawberry Rhubarb

4 cups frozen rhubarb pieces

3 cups frozen strawberries, halved if large

1 tablespoon lemon or orange juice

½ cup granulated sugar

¼ cup plus 1 tablespoon cornstarch

¼ cup brown sugar

¼ teaspoon sea salt

1 teaspoon vanilla extract

½ teaspoon finely grated orange zest (optional)

Bramble Berry

4 cups frozen raspberries

3 cups frozen blackberries

1 tablespoon lemon juice

¾ cup sugar

¼ cup plus 2 tablespoons cornstarch

¼ teaspoon sea salt

1 teaspoon vanilla extract

NOTE: *Apple pie is much better when the filling is made ahead with fresh apples and then frozen (see page 41).*

KEEPING A VEGGIE-SCRAP FREEZER CONTAINER FOR BROTH

When you're cooking real-food meals, it's guaranteed you'll have a lot of veggie scraps that might otherwise end up in the trash or compost. Things such as carrot ends, celery leaves, onion skins, and herb stems have a lot of flavor and nutrition to give and can be frozen to use for making broth later.

I keep a plastic container in the freezer and toss in these odds and ends from my everyday cooking. Once the container is full, it's time to restock my broth supply!

I strive to keep the contents neutral, as I prefer a plain-flavored broth that will bend to whatever I'm making. Besides onions, celery, and carrots, try adding trimmings from leeks, mushrooms, parsnips, scallions, and herbs. I omit strongly flavored veggies such as broccoli, cauliflower, and kale, and members of the nightshade family such as peppers, tomatoes, and potatoes. I like to make the following recipe using the veggies in my scrap container, plus some freshly roasted vegetables.

Roasted Vegetable Broth

A full-flavored broth is the foundation of every great soup or stew, and caramelizing the veggies in the oven before boiling them adds a lot of depth! This recipe is excellent as is and can stand alone, but I often use it as a base, adding in whatever is in my frozen veggie scrap container.

YIELD: 4 CUPS

- 3 large carrots
- 3 celery stalks
- 1 large yellow onion
- 3 peeled garlic cloves
- 1 tablespoon extra-virgin olive oil
- 8 cups water
- 3 parsley sprigs
- 1 bay leaf
- 6 whole peppercorns
- ½ teaspoon sea salt
- Assorted frozen veggie scraps (optional)

1 Preheat the oven to 425°F (220°C).

2 Cut the carrots and celery into 2-inch pieces. Peel the onion and cut it into quarters, reserving any peels that aren't dirty, as they add rich flavor and deep color to broth.

3 Place the carrots, celery, onion, and garlic on a baking pan and toss with the oil. Bake for 40 minutes, or until the veggies are starting to brown.

4 Transfer the roasted veggies to a large pot. Add the water, parsley, bay leaf, peppercorns, and salt, plus the reserved onion skins and any additional frozen veggie scraps, if using. Bring to a boil and simmer for 1 hour.

5 Place a colander over a large bowl and strain out all the vegetables and herbs, collecting the broth in the bowl below.

6 **To freeze:** Cool before freezing. Because it is liquid, broth packs best in rigid containers.

FREEZING PRODUCE FROM A TO Z

❄

APPLES

Autumn is my favorite time of year: crisp air, rustling leaves, cozy sweaters, and apple everything! Each variety of apple has its own flavor notes, so whatever you're making—whether it's pie, applesauce, or even cider—your recipe will benefit from using more than one type of apple to get the most well-rounded flavor.

Freeze Grated Apple!

Freeze individual portions of grated raw apple in silicone molds or ice cube trays for baking or stirring into things such as yogurt and oatmeal.

Freezing Raw Apple Slices

Apple varieties that are dense or crisp, such as Honeycrisp, Gala, and Pink Lady, work best for freezing. Frozen apples have a very similar flavor to fresh, and their softness makes them ideal for cooking and baking.

Prep. Frozen apple peels will become tough and leathery when thawed, especially against the contrast of the softened apple flesh, so peel the apples before you freeze them. Then cut apples into slices about ¼ inch thick. If cut too thick, the apples will take on a squishy water-balloon texture.

Freeze. Apple slices pack best in freezer bags. Because apples will brown when exposed to air, work in batches and get them into the freezer as soon as they are ready.

Special thawing instructions. As the apples thaw, they will release a lot of liquid. Make sure to save this apple juice, as it contains a ton of flavor! The easiest way to collect the juice is to hold the freezer bag over a bowl, snip off a corner, and let the liquid drain out.

Cooking & Baking with Frozen Apple Slices

Adapting your favorite recipes for frozen apples will take a little practice. Most recipes take into account the amount of liquid in an apple, which is contained within a fresh apple's cells. Apples that have been frozen and then thawed release that liquid because their cells have burst.

I generally prefer to let apple slices thaw fully before using them in order to manage the large amount of juice they release. If you use all the juice, your dish may turn out soggy, but if you don't use any, your dish may be bland and dry. The best solution I've found is to pour the juice into a saucepan and simmer until the volume is reduced by about half. Allow the thickened juice to cool before adding it to a recipe.

You can use frozen apple slices in pies, cobblers, and crisps, but these dishes will be significantly better if you make and freeze the filling instead (see page 41).

Making & Freezing
Fresh Raw Apple Cider

There is some debate in the apple world as to what differentiates apple juice from apple cider. Where I live, "cider" is freshly pressed, not heated or filtered, and nonalcoholic. It's tart and sweet and tastes like biting into a freshly picked apple!

For the small-scale preserver, the easiest way to make cider is to use an electric juicer. If you're juicing more than a couple of bushels every year, you might consider a small cider press.

Prep. To juice apples, leave the peels on but remove the cores, and cut the apples into pieces that will fit in your juicer's hopper. Juicing apples produces foam that will rise and sit on top of the juice. This foam is edible, but I prefer to use a slotted spoon to remove it before freezing.

You can also juice apples by freezing and then pressing them with a cider press, a technique I learned in Claude Jolicoeur's book *The New Cider Maker's Handbook*. Freeze the apples whole for 1 week, and then thaw and press them slowly and gently. The cider will be more viscous than fresh cider and have an odd mouthfeel when drunk straight, but it's useful for cooking and baking or turning into hard cider.

Freeze. Because it is liquid, apple cider packs best in rigid containers. Many people save and reuse plastic jugs from juice and vinegar for freezing cider.

Freeze Cider from Your Local Orchard!

Fresh cider from your local orchard typically comes in half- or full-gallon plastic jugs, and it can be frozen directly in these containers. Make sure to pour off some of the cider, leaving about 2 inches of headspace so that when the cider freezes and expands, it doesn't burst the jug.

Apple Pie Filling

My grandma always made the best pie with a flaky lard and butter crust, lots of warm spices, and plenty of love (the secret ingredient!). I've aspired to make pie as good as hers. My version of apple pie filling is perfectly sweet and spiced, with enough sauciness to hold the apples together without being runny. Make sure to use apples that will hold their shape when baked, such as Honeycrisp or Granny Smith, so that you don't end up with an applesauce pie! Use this filling for pie, crisp, or cobbler.

YIELD: FILLING FOR ONE 9-INCH PIE

- 9 cups peeled, sliced apples, ¼–½ inch thick (about 3½ pounds whole)
- 2 tablespoons water
- ½ cup granulated sugar
- ¼ cup firmly packed brown sugar (see Note)
- 3 tablespoons all-purpose flour or gluten-free flour blend
- 1 teaspoon ground cinnamon
- ½ teaspoon sea salt
- ¼ teaspoon grated nutmeg
- ¼ teaspoon ground allspice
- 1 teaspoon vanilla extract

1 Combine the apples and water in a large pot, cover, and place over medium heat. Cook until softened, 16 to 18 minutes, gently folding and stirring the apples with a silicone spatula every few minutes; replace the cover between stirrings.

2 Stir together the granulated sugar, brown sugar, flour, cinnamon, salt, nutmeg, and allspice in a bowl, then stir the mixture into the apples. Cook, stirring continuously, until the apples are surrounded by a thick, gooey sauce, about 2 minutes.

3 Remove from the heat and stir in the vanilla.

4 **To freeze:** Cool before freezing. Apple pie filling packs best in a gallon-size freezer bag.

5 **To thaw:** Thaw overnight in the refrigerator. It's okay to bake this filling into a pie when it is still partially frozen, but it will require additional cooking time.

NOTE: *If you prefer a pie that is less sweet, omit the brown sugar.*

BAKING THE FILLING INTO PIE

When you're ready to bake your filling into a pie, preheat the oven to 425°F (220°C). Transfer the thawed filling to a prepared 9-inch pie shell. Cover with a top crust and pinch the edges together to form the outer lip of the crust. Cut five 2-inch slits in the top to allow steam to escape. Dress up the top crust however you prefer, with an egg-wash or perhaps a sprinkling of sugar. Alternatively, use a lattice or crumble topping. Bake the pie for 20 minutes. Reduce the oven temperature to 375°F (190°C) and bake for 40 to 45 minutes longer, or until the filling looks bubbly and the crust is golden brown. Allow the pie to cool completely before slicing, otherwise it will be runny.

Smooth or Chunky Applesauce

Do you like your applesauce smooth or chunky? This recipe can be adapted either way. If you prefer yours chunky, peel the apples before cooking and then mash lightly. I prefer to leave the peels on because they add extra flavor and fiber (plus it's less work!), but this means the sauce needs to be puréed to break down the skins. I typically freeze my applesauce plain and dress it up with maple syrup and cinnamon upon serving.

YIELD: ABOUT 4 CUPS

8 cups chopped apples (3 to 4 pounds whole; peeled if making chunky)

1 Cover the bottom of a large pot with ⅛ inch of water, then add the apples. Cover and cook over medium heat for 15 minutes.

2 Remove the lid and continue cooking, stirring occasionally, until the apples are soft and easily mashed, about 30 minutes. Apples like to sputter when cooking, so be careful when stirring. Remove from the heat and allow the apples to cool to a safe handling temperature.

3 For smooth applesauce, use an immersion blender or transfer to a countertop blender and blend on high until smooth. Work in batches, if needed. For chunky applesauce, use a handheld masher to gently crush the apples to your desired consistency.

4 **To freeze:** Cool before freezing. Applesauce packs well in bags or rigid containers.

NOTE: *You can use whatever quantity of apples you have on hand; this recipe is easy to scale up or down. If working with a very large quantity, consider using a food mill to purée them, which will also remove the skins so there's no need to peel first.*

Variation: Blackberry Applesauce

Apples and dark berries are great friends! Combine apples with other seasonal flavors (try raspberries, strawberries, or plums) to preserve something extra special. Because blackberries are tart, this applesauce benefits from just a touch of added sugar, although it is optional.

To make, follow the instructions for Smooth or Chunky Applesauce. After step 1, stir in 1 cup fresh or frozen blackberries and ¼ cup sugar or honey, then continue cooking as called for in step 2. Follow the instructions in steps 3 and 4 for puréeing the sauce and freezing.

Orange & Brown Sugar Apple Butter

Apple butter is a thick, intensely flavored, spreadable purée made by cooking apples past the sauce stage until they caramelize. Because the volume reduces so much, this is a good solution if you have a lot of apples and not a lot of freezer space.

YIELD: ABOUT 4 CUPS

- 16 cups chopped apples, cut into 1- to 2-inch pieces (about 6 pounds whole; see Note)
- ¾ cup firmly packed brown sugar
- ½ cup water
- Zest and juice of 1 large orange
- 1 teaspoon vanilla extract
- 1 teaspoon ground cinnamon
- ¼ teaspoon sea salt

1 Combine the apples, brown sugar, water, orange zest and juice, vanilla, cinnamon, and salt in a 6-quart slow cooker. Cover and cook on high for 2 hours.

2 Give the apples a good stir, then cook until they are soft and easily mashed, about 2 hours longer.

3 Allow the apples to cool to a safe handling temperature, then use an immersion blender or transfer to a countertop blender and blend on high until smooth. Work in batches, if needed.

4 Return the puréed apples to the slow cooker and cook on high, uncovered, stirring every hour, until the mixture is so thick that a large scoop of it sticks to the spoon when held upside down, 3 to 4 hours longer. It's okay if the apple butter forms a skin on top between stirrings; just mix it in. Some slow cookers run much hotter than others, so cooking times may vary.

5 **To freeze:** Cool before freezing. Because it is thick, apple butter packs best in rigid containers. A little goes a long way with apple butter, so I prefer to freeze this in small containers.

NOTE: *There's no need to peel the apples for this recipe. If using frozen apples, thaw the apples first and include all the liquid they release, then eliminate the water in step 1.*

Variation: Simple Unsweetened Apple Butter

This simple version is the ideal canvas for making barbecue sauce, pairing with meats and other savory dishes, or using in baked goods. As there are no spices or sugar added, the flavor of the apples really shines!

Follow the instructions for Orange & Brown Sugar Apple Butter, but omit the brown sugar, orange zest and juice, vanilla, and cinnamon.

Fried Apples

Apples fried in butter and sugar until they're tender and syrupy go well with just about any meal. Serve them atop waffles for breakfast, with sandwiches for lunch, or next to pork chops for dinner. You can also turn them into a proper dessert with a scoop of vanilla ice cream.

YIELD: 4 SERVINGS

- 2 tablespoons butter or coconut oil
- 1 quart frozen apple slices (about 4 cups), thawed
- ¼ cup dark maple syrup or firmly packed brown sugar
- ½ teaspoon vanilla extract
- ¼ teaspoon sea salt

1 Melt the butter in a skillet over medium heat. Add the apple slices along with all their liquid.

2 Simmer, stirring frequently, until the apples are cooked through and most of the liquid has evaporated, about 10 minutes.

3 Stir in the maple syrup, vanilla, and salt, and simmer for 3 to 5 minutes longer or until the sauce has thickened.

Apple Cider Donut Cookies

During the harvest season, our favorite local orchard sells fresh apple cider donuts that are rolled in cinnamon sugar and served warm. They go great with a cup of coffee and a hay ride! This is the cookie version—soft and cakey, full of cinnamon, and with a hint of apple from the apple butter. Use plain or spiced apple butter in this recipe.

YIELD: 24 COOKIES

COOKIES

- 10 tablespoons butter, melted
- ½ cup sugar
- 1 egg
- ½ cup frozen apple butter (page 43), thawed
- 1 teaspoon vanilla extract
- 1½ cups all-purpose flour or gluten-free flour blend
- 1 teaspoon baking soda
- 1 teaspoon ground cinnamon
- ½ teaspoon sea salt
- ½ teaspoon ground allspice

COATING

- ¼ cup sugar
- ½ teaspoon ground cinnamon

1 To make the cookies, place the butter and sugar in a large bowl. Using a hand mixer or stand mixer fitted with a paddle attachment, beat together on medium-high speed until combined, about 1 minute.

2 Add the egg, apple butter, and vanilla, and continue beating until fluffy, about 2 minutes. Scrape down the sides and bottom of the bowl with a spatula as needed.

3 Stir together the flour, baking soda, cinnamon, salt, and allspice in a bowl, then add it to the dough mixture and beat on low speed until just combined. Cover and chill the dough in the refrigerator for 2 hours.

4 Preheat the oven to 350°F (180°C). Line a baking pan with parchment paper.

5 To make the coating, combine the sugar and cinnamon in a small bowl.

6 Roll the cookie dough into balls, using about 1½ table-spoons of dough each, then toss them in the cinnamon sugar to coat. Arrange the balls 3 inches apart on the prepared baking pan, then press each one down to flatten it to about ½ inch thick.

7 Bake on the top rack of the oven for 9 to 11 minutes, or until the cookies are set in the middle and just starting to brown. Cool for 5 minutes on the pan, then transfer to a wire rack to cool completely.

ASPARAGUS

Asparagus is the bellwether of spring here, popping up as one of the first foods to harvest and quickly disappearing soon after. Where I come from, wild asparagus grows all over. We hunt for it in fall because its distinct, tall, fernlike fronds give its location away. Once we find where it grows, we come back in spring to harvest it.

Freezing Asparagus Pieces

A notoriously difficult vegetable to preserve, frozen asparagus will be mushy once thawed, so try it in blended soups where its texture disappears into the background.

Prep. Remove the woody bottom part of the spears and cut the asparagus into 2- to 3-inch pieces.

Blanch. Steam blanch (see page 10) thin spears for 2 minutes, medium spears for 3 minutes, and thick spears for 4 minutes, tossing the asparagus around at the halfway mark. Move immediately to an ice bath and chill for 2 minutes. Drain as much water from the asparagus as possible, then transfer to a towel-lined pan to dry.

Freeze. Asparagus packs best in freezer bags.

AVOCADO

You can't always find a ripe avocado when you need one, so keeping a supply stashed in the freezer can be a lifesaver. Here's how to tell if an avocado is ripe: Remove the stem nubbin; it should be a bright spring green color underneath. Squeeze the fruit gently; if it gives just a little, it's ready. Most avocados (including the popular Hass) will be dark-colored when ripe, although some varieties stay green-skinned at maturity.

Freezing Quartered or Mashed Avocado

Once thawed, avocado will start to brown quickly, so use it right away. It will have a slightly translucent quality and be a touch softer than fresh, but it's still delicious. Frozen avocado can be used for topping toast, making guacamole, or transforming into desserts such as pudding or brownies.

Prep. Remove the avocado skin and pit before freezing: Remove the stem nubbin, then cut the avocado in half lengthwise, working around the large pit in the center. Remove the pit and cut each avocado half in half lengthwise again. Peel off the skin and discard. Freezing the avocado in quarters will make it easy to know how much you're using.

For mashed avocado, fill a freezer bag with avocado pieces, remove the air, and seal the bag. Place the bag flat on the counter and gently press down to mash the avocado and spread it out into a flat layer. Mashing it inside the sealed bag will minimize the amount of air the flesh is exposed to and help prevent browning.

Freeze. Flash freeze avocado quarters, then transfer to a freezer bag for storage. Mashed avocado packs best in freezer bags. Because avocados will brown when exposed to air, work quickly and get them into the freezer as soon as they are prepped.

FOR THE TABLE

Homemade Guacamole

I'm famous for my guacamole . . . and by that I mean my friends and family say that mine is the best, and I hold on tightly to that title! I prefer a guacamole where the avocado is the star and the other ingredients enhance its flavor but don't overpower it. If you're one of those folks who isn't fond of cilantro, feel free to leave it out.

YIELD: 6 SERVINGS

- 12 frozen avocado quarters, thawed
- 4 teaspoons lime juice
- ¾ teaspoon sea salt
- 2 jalapeños, cored, deseeded, and diced
- ½ small red onion, finely chopped
- ¼ cup chopped fresh cilantro (optional)

1 Place the avocados, lime juice, and salt in a bowl, and mash them together with a fork.

2 Stir in the jalapeños, onion, and cilantro, if using. Let the guacamole sit for 10 minutes before serving.

Bananas that are slightly green (middle) are my favorite choice for smoothies, and bananas that are sunny yellow and just starting to develop brown spots (right) are best for baking.

BANANAS

Bananas become sweeter and have more banana flavor as they ripen, but they can develop an overpowering and unpleasant taste if they get too brown. For baking, the Goldilocks point is when the peels are sunshine yellow and just starting to develop some brown spots. For making smoothies, I prefer the bananas to be slightly green because they have a lower sugar content and a silkier texture than riper bananas.

Freezing Sliced or Mashed Banana

Prep. If you're not sure how you are going to use your bananas, freeze them in pieces. For smoothies, cut peeled bananas into 1-inch pieces to ensure the blender will be able to handle them. For baking, consider mashing the bananas before freezing, which will take up less space.

Freeze. Flash freeze banana pieces, then transfer to a freezer bag for storage. Mashed bananas pack well in freezer bags or rigid containers. You can also put a banana in its peel directly into the freezer. The peel will turn black, but it does a nice job of protecting the flesh underneath.

"Lazy" Chocolate-Covered Frozen Banana Slices

Chocolate-covered frozen banana slices are a popular treat, but I don't like taking the time to hand dip every single one. This method is ideal for anyone short on time or ambition. Once frozen, bananas have a creamy texture similar to ice cream, and they're extra decadent drizzled with chocolate and peanut butter! Eat these frozen, straight out of the freezer.

YIELD: 9 SERVINGS

  3 medium–large bananas, cut into ½-inch-thick slices

  ⅓ cup chocolate chips (any type)

  1 teaspoon coconut oil

  1 tablespoon peanut butter (optional)

  Toppings: chopped nuts, flaked coconut, sprinkles, crushed freeze-dried berries, pretzel pieces, or graham cracker crumbs (optional)

1 Line a baking pan with parchment paper. Arrange the banana slices on the prepared pan so that they are touching but not overlapping.

2 Combine the chocolate chips and coconut oil in a small glass bowl and microwave on high for 90 seconds or until melted, stopping every 15 seconds to stir. Use a fork to drizzle the melted chocolate back and forth over the banana slices. If using peanut butter, place it in a small glass bowl. Microwave for 30 to 60 seconds, stirring every 15 seconds, until melted and runny. Drizzle the peanut butter on top of the chocolate.

3 If adding toppings, sprinkle them on before the chocolate hardens.

4 **To freeze:** Place the pan in the freezer for 4 hours or up to overnight. Break the banana slices apart and transfer to a freezer container for storage.

Banana-Pineapple-Ginger Smoothie

The coconut milk and banana make this smoothie ridiculously creamy, and the pineapple and fresh ginger taste like sunshine on a tropical beach. I prefer a light coconut milk for this recipe, but feel free to use whatever milk or nondairy alternative you like.

YIELD: 1 SERVING

- 1½ cups frozen banana pieces
- ½ cup frozen pineapple
- 1 cup light coconut milk
- 2 tablespoons raw cashews
- ½ teaspoon grated fresh ginger

Place the banana, pineapple, coconut milk, cashews, and ginger in a blender. Blend on high until smooth, about 30 seconds, and serve immediately.

Flourless Peanut Butter–Banana–Chocolate Chip Muffins

Made with pantry (and freezer) staples and whipped up in the blender, these naturally grain-free muffins come together quickly. The texture is soft and springy—you'd never guess they were made without flour and with only a small amount of sugar. The peanut butter and egg make these fairly high in protein, so they're a satisfying midday snack.

YIELD: 12 MUFFINS

- 1 cup frozen mashed banana, thawed
- 1 cup smooth unsweetened peanut butter
- 3 eggs
- ⅓ cup firmly packed brown sugar
- 1 teaspoon apple cider vinegar
- 1 teaspoon baking soda
- 1 teaspoon vanilla extract
- ¼–½ teaspoon sea salt
- ⅓ cup plus 2 tablespoons semisweet chocolate chips

1 Preheat the oven to 350°F (180°C). Line a standard 12-cup muffin pan with paper liners.

2 Place the banana, peanut butter, eggs, sugar, vinegar, baking soda, and vanilla in a blender or food processor. If your peanut butter is salted, add ¼ teaspoon salt; if it's unsalted, use ½ teaspoon. Blend on high speed until the batter is smooth and uniform, about 30 seconds.

3 Use a spatula to fold in the ⅓ cup chocolate chips.

4 Fill each muffin cup with ¼ cup of batter, then sprinkle the remaining 2 tablespoons chocolate chips evenly over the tops of the muffin cups.

5 Bake for about 20 minutes, or until the tops are turning golden brown and a toothpick inserted in the center of a muffin comes out clean. Cool completely before eating.

Banana Cake with Brown Sugar Frosting

I'll choose a rustic homespun cake over a fancy frilly one any day. This banana cake is lightly sweetened, tender, and remarkably moist thanks to all those bananas. A pillowy brown sugar buttercream frosting is the perfect accompaniment!

YIELD: 12 SERVINGS

CAKE

Cooking spray, for greasing pan

1½ cups frozen mashed banana, thawed

½ cup avocado oil or melted coconut oil

⅓ cup granulated sugar

2 eggs

1 teaspoon vanilla extract

1½ cups all-purpose flour or gluten-free flour blend

2 teaspoons baking soda

½ teaspoon sea salt

⅓ cup chopped walnuts (optional)

FROSTING

¼ cup half-and-half

½ cup firmly packed brown sugar

6 tablespoons butter, at room temperature

1½ cups confectioners' sugar

1 teaspoon vanilla extract

⅛ teaspoon sea salt

1 Preheat the oven to 325°F (160°C). Grease an 8-inch square metal baking pan.

2 To make the cake, place the banana, oil, granulated sugar, eggs, and vanilla in a large bowl. Using a hand mixer or stand mixer fitted with a paddle attachment, beat on medium speed until combined, about 1 minute.

3 Stir together the flour, baking soda, and salt in a bowl, then add it to the batter mixture and beat on low speed until just combined. Fold in the walnuts, if using.

4 Pour the batter into the prepared pan and bake for 35 to 40 minutes, or until a toothpick inserted in the center comes out clean. The cake should be golden brown on the top and around the edges. Let cool.

5 To make the frosting, combine the half-and-half and brown sugar in a small saucepan over low heat. Cook, stirring continuously, until the brown sugar has dissolved, about 5 minutes. Pour the mixture into a small bowl and let cool completely.

6 Place the butter, confectioners' sugar, vanilla, and salt in a large bowl. Using a hand mixer or stand mixer fitted with a paddle attachment, beat on low speed until just combined, then on high speed until fluffy, about 1 minute. Pour in the cooled brown sugar mixture and beat until smooth, about 1 minute longer.

7 Frost the cake and serve.

Use Beets in a Smoothie!

Try adding a few frozen beet chunks to your next smoothie. They add a gorgeous red color, not to mention extra fiber and nutrients!

BEETS

Intensely and beautifully colored, beets have an abundance of nutrients. If you are working through a lot of red beets, consider wearing gloves so your hands don't become stained. And don't discard those beet greens—they can be frozen following the instructions on page 105 for dark leafy greens.

Freezing Beets in All Forms

Beets freeze best when they're fully cooked, not just blanched. Both red and golden beets can be frozen, and their texture holds up remarkably well in the freezer.

Prep. Remove the beet greens, leaving ½ inch of stem still attached to the beet. Small beets can be left whole, but those larger than a baseball should be cut in half. Steam (preferred) or boil beets until fork-tender, about 30 minutes. While still warm, use a paper towel to rub off and remove the skin. Beets can be frozen whole, in halves, cut into smaller pieces, or puréed (which is perfect for making the Seedy Beet Crackers on page 54).

Freeze. Cool before freezing. Beets pack best in freezer bags. Consider flash freezing beet pieces to use in smaller quantities. Puréed beets pack best in rigid containers.

❄ FOR THE FREEZER

Pickled Sliced Beets

Pickled beets are the quintessential farmhouse food. I'm pretty sure you'd find them in just about any old homestead root cellar. Sometimes when I need a quick side dish to serve with dinner, I'll put out a menagerie of pickled items—beets always included. Even after being frozen, pickled beets are velvety smooth with a naturally sweet taste.

YIELD: 3 PINTS

- 2 pounds beets (about 6 medium), cut in half if large
- 1½ cups water
- 1½ cups distilled white vinegar
- ¼ cup apple cider vinegar
- ¼ cup sugar
- 1 teaspoon sea salt

1 Steam or boil the beets until fork-tender, about 30 minutes. While the beets are still warm, use a paper towel to rub off and remove the skin. Cut the beets into ⅛- to ¼-inch-thick slices, then place in a heatproof nonreactive bowl.

2 Combine the water, vinegars, sugar, and salt in a small saucepan. Cook over medium heat, stirring occasionally, until the sugar has dissolved, about 5 minutes.

3 Bring the mixture just to a boil, then pour the hot brine over the beet slices in the bowl. Refrigerate overnight to allow the beets to absorb the pickling brine.

4 **To freeze:** Evenly distribute the beets and their brine into freezer containers and freeze. Because of the brine, pickled beets pack best in rigid containers.

Seedy Beet Crackers

I have it on good authority that even those who don't like beets think these crackers are yummy! The beet flavor in these brilliant red crackers is very mellow, and the crunch factor is high. Sturdy and crisp, pair them with cheese or a heavy dip such as hummus.

YIELD: 8–10 SERVINGS

- ¾ cup all-purpose flour or gluten-free flour blend
- ¼ cup finely ground cornmeal
- ¼ cup pepitas (pumpkin seeds)
- 2 teaspoons poppy seeds
- 2 teaspoons sesame seeds
- ½ teaspoon sea salt
- 1 cup frozen puréed beets (page 53), thawed (see Note)
- 2 tablespoons extra-virgin olive oil
- ½ teaspoon flaky salt

1 Whisk together the flour, cornmeal, pepitas, poppy seeds, sesame seeds, and sea salt in a large bowl.

2 Add the beets and stir until well combined, then stir in the oil; the dough will be thick. Let the mixture sit for 15 minutes to allow the cornmeal to hydrate.

3 Preheat the oven to 350°F (180°C).

4 Divide the dough in half. Cut four pieces of parchment paper to the size of an 18- by 13-inch baking pan (you will need 2 pans for baking). Roll each portion of dough between two sheets of parchment paper until it is a uniform ⅛-inch thickness. The pepitas are a natural rolling guide—don't press so hard that you crack them.

5 Slide the dough, still sandwiched between the parchment paper, onto the baking pans, then peel off the top layer of paper. Use a pizza cutter (or fancy crinkle cutter if you have one!) to score the dough into cracker-size pieces, making sure to cut all the way through the dough. Sprinkle the top of the dough evenly with flaky salt.

6 Bake for 35 to 40 minutes, or until the dough starts to brown around the edges, rotating the pans halfway through baking for a more even doneness.

7 Let the crackers cool, then break apart and store in an airtight container.

NOTE: *If using previously steamed and frozen whole beets, allow to thaw completely. Process the cooked beets in a food processor until they are finely ground, about 60 seconds, then measure out 1 cup.*

BLUEBERRIES

One of my favorite activities every summer is visiting a local U-pick farm and filling buckets full with plump, juicy berries. Of all the berries, blueberries are one of my favorites to process because they're so quick and easy. They're usually not dirt-covered, and they don't have any crevices where bugs can hide!

Freezing Whole Blueberries

Prep. Blueberries don't require any special preparation.

Freeze. Blueberries pack best in freezer bags. There is no need to flash freeze blueberries, as they can be easily separated when frozen together.

Blueberry-Maple Pancake Sauce

This sauce, made of blueberries, butter, and maple syrup, is everything you want on your breakfast cakes. Instead of drizzling it, I serve this sauce in a bowl on the side so I can dunk my pancakes in it—it's that good! Try this on a Dutch baby, waffles, French toast, and, of course, pancakes.

YIELD: ABOUT 3 CUPS

    4 cups fresh blueberries (see Note)

    1 tablespoon water

    ½ cup dark maple syrup

    2 tablespoons butter

1 Combine the blueberries and water in a medium saucepan. Cover and cook over low heat until the blueberries have softened and start to burst, about 10 minutes.

2 Using a handheld masher, gently mash the berries, leaving some whole so that the sauce has texture.

3 Simmer, uncovered, for 5 minutes. Remove from the heat and whisk in the maple syrup and butter.

4 **To freeze:** Cool before freezing. Blueberry sauce packs best in rigid containers.

5 **To heat:** Heat thawed blueberry sauce in a saucepan over low heat and serve warm.

NOTE: *You can also make this sauce with frozen blueberries to eat fresh; just add a few minutes to the cooking time in step 1.*

Instant Blueberry Cheesecake Ice Cream

This is a fun frozen treat that comes together almost magically. The frozen blueberries freeze the cream, turning it into a slushie-ice cream hybrid with a cheesecake twist. The recipe calls for cream cheese and heavy cream, but this technique is widely adaptable to other types of milk or nondairy alternatives.

YIELD: 1 SERVING

- 1 ounce cream cheese, at room temperature (see Note)
- 2 tablespoons confectioners' sugar
- ½ teaspoon vanilla extract
- ¼ cup heavy cream
- ¼ cup very cold water
- 1 cup frozen blueberries

1 Place the cream cheese in a large mug. Add the sugar and vanilla, and stir vigorously with a fork until well combined.

2 Combine the cream and water in a small bowl. Stir one-third of the mixture at a time into the cream cheese, making sure it is completely incorporated before adding the next addition. Adding the liquid in small amounts like this will prevent clumping.

3 Pour the blueberries into the mug and push them down under the liquid. Let the mixture sit undisturbed for 1 minute.

4 Use a spoon to stir the blueberries into the now-frozen milk to create a slushie ice cream. Eat immediately.

NOTE: *If you can't wait for your cream cheese to come to room temperature naturally, place it in a large microwavable mug and microwave it for 5 seconds, no longer, and then proceed with the recipe.*

Instant Blueberry Cheesecake Ice Cream

Blueberry-Matcha Latte Smoothie

Matcha is finely powdered green tea leaves with a stunning vibrant green color that I have always found alluring. While matcha is most commonly served as a warm beverage, it also blends flawlessly into smoothies. Its grounding earthiness pairs especially well with dark berries.

YIELD: 1 SERVING

- 1 cup frozen blueberries
- ¾ cup frozen banana pieces
- 1 cup milk or almond milk
- 1 teaspoon matcha powder
- 1 teaspoon honey (optional)
- ½ teaspoon vanilla extract

Combine the blueberries, banana, milk, matcha, honey, if using, and vanilla in a blender. Blend on high until smooth, about 30 seconds, and serve immediately.

Homestyle Blueberry Muffins

There's nothing better than biting into a buttery homemade blueberry muffin, but baking with frozen blueberries can be tricky. Thawed berries will break into pieces and turn the batter purple. Frozen blueberries will chill the batter and prevent it from rising properly, leaving you with dense baked goods. Fortunately there's a way to work around these problems, and the extra care is worth it for exceptional muffins!

YIELD: 12 MUFFINS

- ½ cup (1 stick) butter, softened
- ¾ cup granulated sugar
- ¼ cup firmly packed brown sugar
- 2 eggs
- 2 teaspoons vanilla extract
- ½ teaspoon almond extract
- 1½ cups all-purpose flour or gluten-free flour blend
- 2 teaspoons baking powder
- ½ teaspoon sea salt
- ½ cup whole or 2% milk
- 1½ cups frozen blueberries

1 Combine the butter and sugars in a large bowl. Using a hand mixer or stand mixer fitted with a paddle attachment, beat on high speed until creamy, about 1 minute.

2 Add the eggs, vanilla, and almond extract, and beat on medium-high speed until fluffy, about 2 minutes. Scrape down the sides and bottom of the bowl with a spatula as needed.

3 Combine the flour, baking powder, and salt in a bowl. Add half of the flour mixture to the butter mixture and beat on low until just combined, about 10 seconds.

4 Add the milk and beat on low until the batter just comes together, about 10 seconds. Add the remaining flour mixture and beat until just mixed together. Do not overmix.

5 Add the frozen blueberries and beat on low speed until they are evenly incorporated.

6 Line a standard 12-cup muffin pan with paper liners. Spoon the batter into the cups, filling each one about three-quarters full. Let the batter rest for 1 hour before baking to allow the blueberries to thaw.

7 Preheat the oven to 400°F (200°C).

8 Bake for 20 to 22 minutes, or until the muffins turn golden and a toothpick inserted in the center of one comes out clean. These muffins are best eaten the same day they are baked. If eating the next day, pop them in the microwave for 5 seconds to soften.

BOK CHOY

Bok choy always makes an appearance in my garden and is one of my favorite stir-fry veggies. It's very sensitive to high temperatures, so when the weather turns hot and the bok choy is threatening to flower and go to seed, I freeze what's left.

Freezing Bok Choy Pieces

Bok choy benefits from being heat-treated before freezing, and I prefer to sauté it rather than blanch it. Thawed bok choy will be limp and a little waterlogged, but it works well in soup or in stir-fry, where its soft texture will disappear into the background.

Prep. Cut or tear the green leafy parts from the white stalks; we'll treat each part differently.

FOR THE WHITE STALKS: Cut into ½-inch pieces. Heat a large pan over medium-high heat. Add oil to the pan (use 1 teaspoon cooking fat for every 2 cups chopped stalks). Add the stalks, being careful not to overcrowd the pan, and sauté, stirring occasionally, until they turn from white to slightly translucent, about 4 minutes. Be careful not to overcook them. Transfer the stalks to a baking pan and spread them out so they cool as quickly as possible.

FOR THE LEAVES: Cut into 1-inch strips. Heat a large pan over medium-high heat. Add oil to the pan (use 1 teaspoon cooking fat for every 2 cups leaves). Add the leaves and cook, stirring frequently, until they are just wilted, about 2 minutes. Transfer the leaves to a baking pan and spread them out so that they cool as quickly as possible.

Freeze. Bok choy packs well in freezer bags or rigid containers. I like to put a mixture of stalk pieces and green leaves in each container.

BROCCOLI

People often romance homegrown tomatoes, but have you ever compared homegrown broccoli to store-bought? An underrated vegetable indeed, homegrown broccoli is dark green, robustly flavored, and worthy of some freezer space! I find myself growing more every year so that there's plenty for fresh eating all summer and plenty for the freezer too.

Freezing Broccoli Pieces

Prep. Remove any outer leaves still attached, cut the broccoli into large bite-size florets, and cut the thick stem into 1-inch pieces. The stem will get woody toward the bottom, but it is tender toward the top.

Blanch. Steam blanch (preferred; see page 10) for 4 minutes, tossing the broccoli around at the 2-minute mark. Alternatively, blanch for 3 minutes in boiling water

(see page 12). Move immediately to an ice bath and chill for 2 minutes. Drain as much water from the broccoli as possible, then transfer to a towel-lined pan to cool and dry.

Freeze. Broccoli packs best in freezer bags. Consider flash freezing broccoli florets to use in smaller quantities.

Broccoli Cheese Soup

Like comfort in a bowl, this soup is loaded with broccoli in a velvety, cheesy broth. There's no skimping on the cheese or broccoli here! Add a slice of sourdough or Leftover Mashed Potato Quick Bread (page 154) for dipping and you've got a hearty meal.

YIELD: 4 SERVINGS

- 4 tablespoons butter
- ½ medium yellow onion, finely diced
- 1 large carrot, grated
- 2 garlic cloves, minced
- ¼ cup all-purpose flour or gluten-free flour blend
- 2 cups chicken broth
- 1½ cups water
- ¼ teaspoon freshly ground black pepper
- ⅛ teaspoon crushed red pepper
- ⅛ teaspoon grated nutmeg
- 3 cups frozen broccoli, thawed
- 1 cup half-and-half
- 6 ounces medium cheddar cheese, shredded
- ¼ cup grated Parmesan cheese
- Sea salt

1 Melt the butter in a medium pot over medium heat. Add the onion and carrot, and sauté, stirring occasionally, until tender, about 7 minutes.

2 Add the garlic and flour, and cook, stirring frequently, for 3 minutes longer.

3 Pour in the broth and water, then stir in the black pepper, crushed red pepper, and nutmeg.

4 Finely chop the broccoli, leaving a few larger pieces for texture, and toss that into the pot as well. Bring to a boil and simmer gently until the broccoli is tender, about 12 minutes.

5 Reduce the heat to low and stir in the half-and-half and cheeses.

6 Because some broths are saltier than others, taste the soup and add salt if necessary. I typically add about 1 teaspoon salt.

Caesar Roasted Broccoli

In this twist on an old favorite, crispy roasted broccoli is tossed with creamy Caesar dressing and topped with lots of crunchy croutons and plenty of Parmesan cheese. Use your favorite Caesar dressing—either from scratch or from a bottle. If you have a larger crowd to feed, this recipe will easily scale up.

YIELD: 3-4 SERVINGS

> 5 cups frozen broccoli, thawed (see Note)
>
> 1½ tablespoons extra-virgin olive oil or avocado oil
>
> ¼ teaspoon sea salt
>
> 2 tablespoons Caesar dressing
>
> ½ cup croutons
>
> ¼ cup grated Parmesan cheese

1 Preheat the oven to 425°F (220°C).

2 Place the thawed broccoli in a colander to drain any excess liquid, then transfer the broccoli to a clean tea towel to further remove moisture. This will help it become crispy.

3 Pile the broccoli on a large baking pan and toss it with the oil and salt. Spread into a single layer.

4 Bake for 20 to 25 minutes, or until brown and crispy on the bottom.

5 Place the broccoli in a serving bowl, drizzle with the dressing, and toss gently. Lightly crush the croutons and sprinkle them over the top along with the Parmesan.

NOTE: *If your broccoli was flash frozen in pieces, you could cook it from frozen. Follow the directions above but add an extra 3 to 4 minutes of cooking time.*

Variation: Simple Roasted Broccoli

Roasted broccoli is so crispy, toasty, and nutty that even those who do not delight in eating green vegetables will enjoy it!

For plain roasted broccoli, follow steps 1 through 4 for Caesar Roasted Broccoli. Omit the Caesar dressing, croutons, and Parmesan cheese.

CABBAGE

Cabbage is such an old-fashioned and charming vegetable. It has been grown and preserved for ages and comes in many shapes, sizes, and leaf textures—all of which can be frozen.

Freezing Cabbage Pieces

Frozen cabbage will be limp but slightly crisp when thawed, so use it for anything cooked.

Prep. Cut the cabbage away from its core, then chop it into large bite-size pieces.

Blanch. Steam blanch (preferred; see page 10) for 2 minutes, tossing the cabbage around at the 1-minute mark.

Alternatively, blanch for 90 seconds in boiling water (see page 12). Cabbage doesn't need an ice bath. Drain as much water as possible, then spread the warm cabbage on a towel-lined pan to cool and dry.

Freeze. Cabbage packs best in freezer bags.

Dill pickle kraut (front) and traditional sauerkraut (back) at the start of fermentation.

INTRO TO FERMENTING & FREEZING SAUERKRAUT

Whether or not to freeze lacto-fermented foods is a debated topic, with those in opposition arguing that freezing kills some the beneficial bacteria. Homemade sauerkraut can contain an impressive diversity of beneficial bacteria, and it is likely that at least some of them do survive. While I agree that refrigeration is the best way to store kraut, there *are* compelling reasons to stash it in the freezer. Lack of fridge space and wanting a foolproof way to ensure it keeps long term are two that come to mind. Other beneficial components, such as vitamins, minerals, and fiber, are preserved in the freezer. Thawed sauerkraut will be slightly less crunchy than fresh, but it will taste equally delicious.

Fermentation Basics

- Start with organic produce, because conventional cabbage may have been sprayed with bacteria-killing chemicals that will prevent fermentation.

- Use good-quality sea salt. Don't use iodized salt, as it can stall fermentation. The salt will help draw the water out of the cabbage to form the brine.

- Make sure anything that comes in contact with the fermenting vegetables is nonreactive; glass and lead-free ceramic are the best choices for vessels.

- Weigh your ingredients for the best possible outcome. The cabbage should be weighed after it is shredded.

- Use a fermentation lid (known as an airlock) to allow gases from inside the jar to escape and prevent air and contaminants from getting in.

- Use fermentation weights to keep the cabbage submerged underneath the brine and thus prevent mold growth. Fermentation weights come in different styles, such as stainless steel springs and heavy pieces of ceramic.

Sauerkraut

The process of turning cabbage into sauerkraut feels almost miraculous. It's truly amazing to take so few ingredients and to turn them into something so versatile, nutritious, and enjoyable. Pile that tangy kraut on anything and everything—try kielbasa or bratwursts, corned beef and potatoes, grilled sandwiches with melty Swiss cheese, or even eggs. At my house, we love using an old-fashioned "kraut cutter" to shred the cabbage, but a knife works too—just cut the cabbage as thinly as possible. A box grater will create too fine a shred.

YIELD: ABOUT 8 CUPS

- 4 pounds finely shredded cabbage, outer leaves removed and one reserved
- 2 tablespoons white or gray sea salt

1 Place the shredded cabbage in a large bowl and sprinkle the salt over the top.

2 With clean hands, toss the cabbage around to evenly distribute the salt. Massage the cabbage for 3 minutes, squeezing it to help draw out the water.

3

3 Let the cabbage rest for 15 minutes, then massage it again for 3 minutes. You should see a lot of liquid collecting in the bottom of the bowl.

4 Let the cabbage rest for 5 minutes, then pack it into a half-gallon jar until the jar is about one-third full. A canning funnel will minimize mess while filling the jar. Alternatively, use two quart jars.

5 Using a wooden spoon, your fist, or a fermenting tamper, as shown, gently but firmly pack down the cabbage in the jar. Fill the jar another third of the way and pack the material down again, then fill it the rest of the way. If needed, add leftover brine so that the cabbage is fully submerged under the liquid. Make sure there is less than 1 inch of headspace at the top of the jar.

5

6 Cut or fold the reserved cabbage leaf to the approximate diameter of the jar opening, then use it to cover the shredded cabbage. This will help keep it submerged.

7

7 Add a fermentation weight. Use a slotted spoon to remove any small pieces of cabbage that inevitably escape and float at the top.

Recipe continues on next page

Sauerkraut, *continued*

8 Secure the airlock on the jar, then place the jar on a plate to catch any juice that may leak out while the cabbage ferments. Let the cabbage sit at room temperature for 7 to 14 days, or until the cabbage is pleasantly sour. Warmer temperatures will cause the cabbage to ferment faster, so keep an eye on it. As it ferments, the good bacteria convert the vegetable starches into lactic acid. Bubbles, color changes, and cloudy brine are all normal.

9 **To freeze:** Evenly distribute the sauerkraut and its brine among freezer containers and freeze immediately. Sauerkraut packs well in freezer bags or rigid containers.

10 **To thaw:** Do not use heat to thaw sauerkraut, as this will destroy the beneficial bacteria.

Variation: Dill Pickle Kraut

This kraut combines two favorite ferments into one! It has the zippy flavor of a classic sauerkraut plus the brininess of traditionally fermented garlic dills.

Follow the instructions for making Sauerkraut above, but in step 1 use 3 pounds finely shredded cabbage, 1 pound thinly sliced cucumber, 4 cloves sliced garlic, 2 tablespoons chopped fresh dill, and 2 tablespoons white or gray sea salt.

▯ FOR THE TABLE

Cabbage Roll Soup

Traditional cabbage rolls are made by stuffing blanched cabbage leaves with a mixture of ground beef and rice, then they are topped with tomato sauce and baked. Thankfully this soup is much easier and just as tasty!

YIELD: 6–8 SERVINGS

2 tablespoons butter, extra-virgin olive oil, or lard
2 pounds ground beef or ground turkey
1 medium yellow onion, diced
3 celery stalks, diced
2 large carrots, diced
2 garlic cloves, minced
4 cups chicken broth
1 (14.5-ounce) can diced tomatoes
3 tablespoons tomato paste
¼ teaspoon freshly ground black pepper
4 cups frozen chopped cabbage, thawed
   Sea salt
¼ cup chopped fresh parsley
3 cups cooked white rice, for serving

1 Heat 1 tablespoon of the butter in a skillet over medium heat. Add the beef and cook, stirring and chopping it into small pieces, until browned, about 10 minutes. Drain any excess fat, and set the meat aside.

2 Heat the remaining 1 tablespoon butter in a large pot over medium heat. Add the onion and celery, and sauté until tender, about 7 minutes.

3 Stir in the cooked meat along with the carrots, garlic, chicken broth, diced tomatoes, tomato paste, and pepper, and simmer, uncovered, until the carrots are tender, about 15 minutes.

4 Stir in the cabbage and simmer for 5 minutes longer. Because some broths are saltier than others, taste the soup and add salt if necessary. I typically add about 1 teaspoon salt.

5 Remove from the heat and stir in the parsley. Serve, topping each bowl with a portion of rice.

Old-Fashioned Freezer Slaw

The secret to making an excellent freezer slaw is to finely grate the cabbage. This helps conceal the limp texture of raw frozen cabbage. The sweet tanginess of this slaw goes well with anything—from barbecue to fried chicken. Note that the mayonnaise is added *after* the slaw is thawed, right before serving. This recipe makes 1 quart of slaw, but you can easily scale it up to make a larger batch.

YIELD: 4 CUPS

FOR FREEZING

- ¼ cup white wine vinegar
- 3 tablespoons sugar
- ¾ teaspoon sea salt
- ⅛ teaspoon celery seed
- 5 cups lightly packed finely grated cabbage (about ½ large head; see Note)
- ¼ cup grated carrot

FOR SERVING

- 2 tablespoons mayonnaise

1 Whisk together the vinegar, sugar, salt, and celery seed in a large bowl. Let the mixture sit for 10 minutes, stirring occasionally to help dissolve the sugar.

2 Fold in the cabbage and carrot, and let the slaw sit for 10 minutes longer.

3 **To freeze:** Divide the slaw between two containers and freeze immediately. Slaw packs well in freezer bags or rigid containers.

4 **To thaw:** Thaw overnight in the refrigerator. Drain any excess liquid and stir in the mayonnaise just before serving.

NOTE: *The easiest way to finely grate a cabbage is to cut it in half through the stem, leaving the stem intact on each side. This helps hold the cabbage together. Press the cut side of the cabbage against the box grater when grating.*

Sweet & Sour Red Cabbage

This sprightly red cabbage is a popular German side dish that is cooked low and slow until tender, then served alongside roasted meat. It is buttery and slightly sweet and has a good zing from the vinegar. The cooking process softens the cabbage so it doesn't suffer any textural change in the freezer.

YIELD: ABOUT 3 CUPS

- 2 tablespoons butter
- ½ large yellow onion, diced
- 1 cup water
- 2 tablespoons firmly packed brown sugar
- 2 tablespoons red wine vinegar
- 1 teaspoon sea salt
- 1 bay leaf
- 8 cups thinly sliced red cabbage (about 1 medium whole)
- 1 apple, diced

1 Melt the butter in a medium pot over medium heat. Add the onion and sauté until tender, about 7 minutes.

2 Add the water, sugar, vinegar, salt, and bay leaf, and then stir in the cabbage and apple, and bring to a simmer.

3 Cover and cook, stirring occasionally, until the cabbage is tender and the liquid is reduced, about 1 hour. Uncover and continue cooking until any liquid on the bottom of the pot has evaporated, about 10 minutes longer.

4 **To freeze:** Cool before freezing. Sweet-and-sour cabbage packs well in freezer bags or rigid containers.

CARROTS

It's always thrilling to harvest carrots! Each carrot emerges as a surprise from under the ground, and there's nothing like the satisfaction of hearing that "pop" as the root lets go of the earth. Carrots are an incredibly versatile veggie, and my household makes sure to have a healthy supply on hand. When freezing carrots in any form, it's your choice whether to peel them or not.

Freezing Shredded Carrots

Shredded carrots can be frozen raw or blanched. Once thawed, raw carrots will have more carrot flavor but will be slightly darkened. Blanched carrots will keep for longer in the freezer and retain a brighter orange color but will have less carrot flavor.

Prep. Whole carrots can be shredded with a box grater or in a food processor with the shredding disc attachment.

Blanch. If blanching, steam blanch (see page 10) for 1½ minutes, tossing the carrots around at the 45-second mark. Steam only about 2 cups shredded carrots at a time so that they cook evenly. Do not place in an ice bath. Spread the warm carrots on a pan to cool and dry.

Freeze. Shredded carrots pack well in freezer bags or rigid containers. Consider freezing smaller portions in a silicone mold.

Freezing Carrot Coins

Frozen carrot coins are an easy addition to soup, and they make for a quick vegetable side dish—try them topped with butter and dill. They will be soft when thawed, but if cooked gently they won't turn to mush.

Prep. Cut carrots into rounds that are approximately ¼ inch thick.

Blanch. Steam blanch (preferred; see page 10) for 3 minutes, tossing the carrots around at the 90-second mark. Alternatively, blanch for 2 minutes in boiling water (see page 12). Move immediately to an ice bath and chill for 3 minutes. Drain as much water from the carrots as possible, then transfer to a towel-lined pan to cool and dry.

Freeze. Carrot coins pack best in freezer bags.

Honey-Butter Carrot Mash

Move over mashed potatoes! Just kidding, you can't beat mashed potatoes . . . but silky mashed carrots with a touch of butter and honey to bring out their natural sweetness will have you going back for seconds. It's important to note that the cream (which is optional or can be substituted with coconut milk) is added when the carrots are thawed and heated for serving.

YIELD: ABOUT 3 CUPS

FOR FREEZING

6 medium carrots (about 1 pound)

2 tablespoons butter

1 tablespoon honey

½ teaspoon sea salt

⅛ teaspoon freshly ground black pepper

FOR SERVING

¼ cup heavy cream or coconut milk (optional)

1 Cut the carrots into approximately 2-inch pieces and steam until tender, about 30 minutes.

2 Transfer the carrots to a food processor. Add the butter, honey, salt, and pepper. Process the carrots until smooth, about 60 seconds.

3 **To freeze:** Cool before freezing. Carrot mash packs well in freezer bags or rigid containers.

4 **To serve:** Combine the thawed carrot mash and cream, if using, in a saucepan and cook over low heat, stirring frequently, until heated through, about 7 minutes. Use a whisk to give the carrot mash a final whip before serving.

Carrot-Coconut Almond Flour Muffins

A more nutrition-centered version of carrot cake, these muffins are higher in protein from the almond flour and eggs and are loaded with carrots, coconut, and cinnamon. Baked goods made with almond flour always stay moist and tender, so they're my favorite to pack for traveling, camping, or long car rides.

YIELD: 9 MUFFINS

- 2 cups finely ground blanched almond flour
- 1 teaspoon ground cinnamon
- ½ teaspoon baking soda
- ¼ teaspoon ground ginger
- ¼ teaspoon sea salt
- 3 eggs
- 2 tablespoons coconut oil, melted
- ⅓ cup dark maple syrup or honey
- ½ teaspoon vanilla extract
- ½ teaspoon almond extract
- 1 cup frozen shredded carrots, thawed
- ¼ cup finely shredded unsweetened coconut
  Sliced almonds, for topping (optional)

1 Preheat the oven to 350°F (180°C). Line a standard 12-cup muffin pan with 9 paper liners.

2 Whisk together the flour, cinnamon, baking soda, ginger, and salt in a large bowl.

3 Stir in the eggs, coconut oil, maple syrup, vanilla, and almond extract, then fold in the carrots and coconut.

4 Fill the muffin cups about two-thirds full with the batter and sprinkle the tops with sliced almonds, if using. Bake for about 25 minutes, or until a toothpick inserted in the center of a muffin comes out clean.

Variation: Chai Carrot Muffins

These delightful muffins are made with spices traditionally found in chai tea. In addition to the cinnamon and ginger already called for in the recipe, add ¼ teaspoon ground cardamom, ¼ teaspoon grated nutmeg, and ⅛ teaspoon ground cloves in step 2.

CAULIFLOWER

A Cinderella story if there ever was one, what once appeared as just an average veggie is now prized for its ability to transform into everything from rice to pizza crust. And we love it for that! Frozen cauliflower florets are useful, or try freezing cauliflower in some of the following versatile and interesting ways.

Freezing Cauliflower Florets

Prep. Cut cauliflower into large bite-size florets, and cut the stems into 1-inch pieces. The stem will get woody toward the bottom, but it is tender toward the top.

Blanch. Steam blanch (preferred; see page 10) for 4 minutes, tossing the cauliflower around at the 2-minute mark. Alternatively, blanch for 3 minutes in boiling water (see page 12). Immediately transfer the blanched

cauliflower to an ice bath and chill for 3 minutes. Drain as much water from the cauliflower as possible, then transfer to a towel-lined pan to cool and dry.

Freeze. Cauliflower florets pack best in freezer bags.

One large head of fresh cauliflower yields roughly 5 cups of florets or 1½ to 2 cups of frozen purée.

Freezing Cauliflower Rice

Prep. Cut the cauliflower into florets, and place them in a food processor. Pulse until the cauliflower is the size of rice. Err on the side of the pieces being too large rather than too small.

Parcook. Place 4 cups riced cauliflower into a medium pot along with ¼ cup water. Cover and cook over medium-high heat for 3 minutes, stirring every minute and replacing the cover between stirrings. Do not use an ice bath. Spread the warm cauliflower rice on a baking pan to cool and dry.

Freeze. Cauliflower rice packs well in freezer bags or rigid containers.

Special instructions. Thaw the cauliflower rice, then place it in a fine-mesh sieve to drain any excess water. Heat a small amount of oil in a skillet, add the cauliflower rice, and sauté until just tender, about 4 minutes; do not overcook.

Freezing Cauliflower Purée

Puréed cauliflower can be dolled up with butter and cream for a low-carb mashed potato substitute, used as a thickener for soups, or made into Cauliflower Dumplings (page 74)—my personal favorite!

Prep. Cut the cauliflower into large bite-size florets, and cut the stem into 1-inch pieces. The stem will get woody toward the bottom, but it is tender toward the top. Steam the cauliflower until tender, about 20 minutes.

Use a food processor to purée the cauliflower until smooth, working in batches if needed. Alternatively, use a handheld masher for chunkier mashed cauliflower.

Freeze. Cool before freezing. Puréed cauliflower packs well in freezer bags or rigid containers.

Add Cauliflower to Smoothies!

It sounds odd, but frozen cauliflower will mysteriously disappear into the background when blended with fruit, while still bringing along its nutrient content.

Cauliflower Dumplings

You will be amazed at how much cauliflower is packed into these pillowy soft dumplings. While they're lovely in soup, my favorite way to eat these dumplings is fried in butter until golden brown. Because they can go directly from the freezer into boiling water and are ready in mere minutes, they're a handy time-saver in the kitchen. Just be careful to wring out most of the water from the cauliflower purée before freezing. This is a critical step in making sure the dumplings hold together when boiled.

YIELD: 4–6 SERVINGS

- 2 cups puréed cauliflower (page 73), cooled
- 1 egg
- ¾ cup all-purpose flour or gluten-free flour blend, plus more as needed
- ½ teaspoon sea salt
- ⅛ teaspoon freshly ground black pepper

1 Line a medium bowl or pot with a thin tea towel. Place the puréed cauliflower in the towel, then gather up the towel to form a ball. Twist and tighten the top of the towel with one hand while using your other hand to squeeze the liquid out of the cauliflower ball. Squeeze it firmly, but not so hard that the cauliflower pushes through the fabric. Keep squeezing until no more streams of liquid come out and you've released nearly 1 cup of liquid. Discard the liquid.

2 Place the cauliflower in a bowl, then mix in the egg. Stir in the flour, salt, and pepper. The dough will be soft and slightly tacky. If the dough is still extremely sticky, add up to 1 tablespoon of additional flour.

3 Refrigerate the dough for 2 hours.

4 **To freeze:** Line a baking pan with parchment paper. Scoop the raw dough by the teaspoonful onto the prepared pan in a single layer, making sure the dumplings do not touch each other. Flash freeze, then transfer the dumplings to a freezer bag for storage.

5 **To heat:** Do not thaw. Drop frozen dumplings into a large pot of boiling water and cook until they all float to the top, 4 to 5 minutes. If using in soup, cook the dumplings in boiling water first and not directly in the broth.

NOTE: *To make these dumplings fresh, omit the freezing step and simply drop the fresh dough by the teaspoonful right into boiling water. Cook for 3 to 4 minutes, or until they all float.*

1

CELERY

Because it's full of so much flavor, homegrown celery is my favorite frozen vegetable for adding to soups, stews, and broth. I always have a few celery plants tucked into the corner of the garden for fresh eating during the growing season and for freezing to have on hand for the soup season ahead.

Freezing Celery Pieces

Frozen celery is best in dishes that are cooked or where the texture will go unnoticed. Thawed celery will be soft, but it will still have good flavor. Use thawed celery pieces in soup or chopped finely for tuna salad, but don't put it on a fresh lettuce salad.

Prep. Remove the leaves and put them aside in your frozen veggie scrap bin (see page 35) for future broth. Celery can be frozen in 4-inch pieces (my preference because they have less surface area and are therefore less prone to freezer burn) or in ½-inch pieces, which are handy for throwing right into soup without thawing first.

Blanch. Steam blanch (see page 10) ½-inch celery pieces for 2 minutes, tossing them around at the 1-minute mark. Steam blanch 4-inch pieces for 3 minutes, tossing them around at the 90-second mark. Do not use an ice bath. Spread the warm celery on a towel-lined pan to cool and dry.

Freeze. Flash freeze celery, then transfer to a freezer bag for storage. Celery packs best in freezer bags.

CHERRIES

Every summer we order a big box of sweet cherries, and I can't help but marvel at how they look like glowing jewels! We eat them fresh until we can't bear to look at another one, then we preserve the rest for winter. Tart and sweet cherries can both be frozen. While they are typically interchangeable in recipes—with a few tweaks—they each excel at different things. Tart cherries provide that classic cherry pie taste (see page 34), and sweet cherries have a deep, sweet flavor that is well suited for raw preparations such as blended drinks.

Freezing Whole Cherries

Prep. Both sweet and tart cherries should be pitted before freezing. There are many creative ways to pit cherries, but I like the simplicity of a handheld cherry pitter tool. Whichever technique you choose, be prepared to get messy, as ripe cherries will spray juice all over!

Freeze. Cherries pack best in freezer bags. Unless very juicy, there is no need to flash freeze cherries, as they can be easily separated when frozen together.

Chocolate-Covered Sweet Cherries

Who doesn't love a plump sweet cherry wrapped in a layer of decadent dark chocolate? Rather than dipping each cherry individually, I tumble pitted cherries in melted chocolate—this way they're poppable straight from the freezer, and I don't have to worry about eating around a pit. Keep these on hand for whenever you need a quick and healthy chocolate treat.

YIELD: ABOUT 2 CUPS

> 2 cups fresh sweet cherries, at room temperature
>
> ½ cup dark chocolate chips, melted

1 Line a baking pan with parchment paper.

2 If the cherries have condensation, dry them off with a paper towel. Remove the stems and pit the cherries. Place them on a paper towel to soak up moisture from the cherry juice. It's important that the cherries be dry.

3 Place the cherries in a large bowl and pour the melted chocolate over them. Using a silicone spatula, quickly fold the cherries into the chocolate, evenly coating them. The chocolate will start to seize and harden when it comes in contact with the moisture in the cherries, but if you work swiftly, you will get them coated before this happens. The chocolate will appear fudgy.

4 While the chocolate is still soft, arrange the cherries in a single layer on the prepared pan.

5 **To freeze:** Flash freeze the chocolate-covered cherries, then transfer to a freezer bag for storage.

NOTE: *Do not double this recipe. If working with a larger quantity of cherries, make only one recipe's worth at a time, and start with a fresh, clean bowl for each batch.*

Cherry Butter

If you're fortunate enough to have a surplus of sweet cherries, a spectacular way to preserve them is to make a luscious cherry butter. This spread is thick and sweet with concentrated cherry flavor—try it on toast or mixed into plain applesauce. My favorite use for cherry butter is swirled into a bowl of warm oatmeal, then drizzled with cream.

YIELD: ABOUT 2 CUPS

> 6 cups pitted sweet cherries (about 2½ pounds whole)
>
> ½ cup water
>
> ⅛ teaspoon sea salt

1 Combine the cherries, water, and salt in a medium pot over medium heat. Bring to a gentle simmer and cook, stirring occasionally, until all the liquid on the bottom of the pan has evaporated, about 1½ hours.

2 Allow the cherries to cool to a safe handling temperature, then transfer to a countertop blender and blend on high until smooth.

3 **To freeze:** Cool before freezing. Because it is thick, cherry butter packs best in rigid containers. A little goes a long way with cherry butter, so I prefer to freeze this in small containers.

10-Minute Vanilla-Cherry Chia Jam

Unlike most preserves, chia jam requires only a short cooking time, which means the cherries retain their fresh flavor. Chia seeds have the unique ability to "gel," and when added to fruit, they thicken it. Because the chia seeds provide the jam factor here, we don't need copious amounts of sugar, pectin, or a long cooking time to make the jam set. This jam is best suited for making and eating fresh and not for freezing.

YIELD: ABOUT 1 CUP

2 cups frozen pitted sweet cherries, thawed

2 tablespoons water

1 tablespoon sugar (optional)

2 teaspoons lemon juice

2 tablespoons chia seeds

1 teaspoon vanilla extract

1 Combine the cherries, water, sugar (if using), and lemon juice in a medium saucepan over medium heat. Bring to a gentle simmer, then cook, stirring occasionally, until the cherries are tender, about 10 minutes.

2 Remove the pan from the heat. Using a handheld masher, mash the cherries, breaking them into smaller pieces.

3 Stir in the chia seeds and vanilla, then transfer the mixture to a pint jar.

4 Refrigerate for 1 hour before serving to cool the fruit and to give the chia seeds time to gel.

TIP: *You can make chia jam with other fruits as well. Follow the same directions and general ratio of fruit to chia seeds listed above and sweeten to taste. Try it with blueberries, strawberries, raspberries, or blackberries.*

Tart Cherry Oatmeal Bars

I love cherry pie (to be honest, I love all pie), but I think I like these cherry bars even better! The perfectly sweet-tart cherry pie filling is delightful sandwiched between layers of buttery oatmeal shortbread crust. These bars are simple to make and absolutely worth all that time spent pitting.

YIELD: 12–16 SERVINGS

FILLING

3 cups frozen pitted tart cherries

⅔ cup granulated sugar

3 tablespoons cornstarch

1 tablespoon lemon juice

1 tablespoon water

BASE AND TOPPING

¾ cup all-purpose flour or gluten-free flour blend

⅔ cup old-fashioned oats

½ cup firmly packed brown sugar

½ teaspoon baking powder

½ teaspoon sea salt

½ cup (1 stick) cold butter, cut into small pieces

1 teaspoon vanilla extract

1 To make the filling, combine the cherries and granulated sugar in a medium saucepan over low heat. Cook, stirring continuously, until the cherries have thawed and released their juices, about 5 minutes. Bring to a boil, then simmer gently until the cherries are tender, about 10 minutes longer.

2 Reduce the heat to low, and use a handheld masher to break the cherries into smaller pieces.

3 Mix together the cornstarch, lemon juice, and water in a small bowl. Slowly add the cornstarch mixture to the pan, whisking continuously. Increase the heat to medium and continue stirring until the cherry mixture has thickened considerably, about 1 minute. Set aside to cool for 20 minutes.

4 Preheat the oven to 350°F (180°C). Line an 8-inch square baking pan with parchment paper: Cut two strips that fit snuggly inside the bottom of the pan and up the sides, and overlap them going in opposite directions.

5 To make the base and topping, combine the flour, oats, brown sugar, baking powder, and salt in a large bowl. Add the butter. Using your hands, rub the butter into the dry ingredients until it is the size of peas and the mixture sticks together in a clump when you squeeze it. Stir in the vanilla.

6 Reserve ¾ cup of the base and topping mixture, then evenly press the rest of the mixture into the bottom of the prepared pan. Pack it down firmly to form the base crust.

7 Spread the cherry mixture in an even layer on top of the crust, then crumble the reserved base and topping mixture evenly over the top.

8 Bake for 45 to 50 minutes, until the top crust is browning around the edges. Cool completely, and then use the parchment paper to help lift the bars out of the pan for cutting.

CITRUS

Citrus season is something I look forward to every year. It works out well that I'm always craving extra vitamin C when the oranges and grapefruits start rolling in. Oranges, lemons, limes, and grapefruits can be frozen in a variety of ways. The one exception is navel oranges, which, according to the USDA, contain a higher amount of a compound called limonin, which turns bitter after the oranges are juiced or frozen.

Freezing Citrus Segments, Wedges, and Slices

Peeled segments work well in smoothies, and wedges or slices can be added to ice water, served on the plate alongside a meal, baked on top of fish, or used for garnishing cocktails.

Citrus can also be frozen whole or in halves, which is perfect for uses such as stuffing inside a whole chicken before baking. However, if the intent is to juice the citrus after it's frozen, it is better to juice first and freeze the juice.

Prep. For citrus segments, peel off the outer rind and remove as much of the white pith as you care to. The pith of grapefruit is often bitter, but in other types of citrus it's bland; pith contains fiber but no real flavor. Citrus can be frozen as individual segments (this is best if they will ultimately be blended) or as larger clusters of segments. For citrus wedges, leave the rind on and cut the fruit into wedges. For citrus slices, leave the rind on and cut into rounds about ⅛ inch thick.

Freeze. Flash freeze peeled citrus segments and clusters of segments, wedges, or slices, then transfer to a freezer bag for storage.

Freezing Fresh Citrus Juice

Thawed citrus juice can be used wherever fresh citrus juice is called for—it's great for drinking or making cocktails.

Prep. Use a handheld reamer or electric citrus juicer to get the highest yield of juice. I prefer to keep the pulp because it adds extra fiber, but you can remove it by pouring the juice through a fine-mesh sieve. Remove any seeds from the juice before freezing.

Freeze. Because it is liquid, citrus juice packs best in rigid containers. Consider freezing smaller portions in a silicone mold.

Freezing Citrus Zest

Zest is the outermost, colorful peel of a citrus fruit. It contains essential oils and so much flavor! The zest is much easier to remove when the fruit is intact, so always zest your fruit before slicing or juicing.

Prep. Use a rasp grater, citrus zester, vegetable peeler, or sharp paring knife. The important thing is not to include any of the white pith underneath the rind.

Freeze. Place finely grated zest in a silicone mold or ice cube tray, then add a small amount of citrus juice or water to help hold it together. Flash freeze large pieces of zest, for example those removed with a peeler or knife, and transfer to a freezer bag to store.

Freeze Kumquats!

Because kumquats can be eaten whole, rind and all, they can be frozen without peeling.
Cut each one in half and remove the seeds (there are usually three or four). Flash freeze, then transfer to a freezer container for storage. Use them for adding flavor and vitamin C to your smoothies!

Honey Lemonade Concentrate

Every year our local beekeepers club has a booth at the county fair selling lemonade made with locally produced honey. The lemonade is always a big hit, and it's a fantastic opportunity to educate the public about honey bees. Just thaw this concentrate and mix with water for instant lemonade—it's very restorative on a hot day.

YIELD: 2 CUPS CONCENTRATE, TO MAKE 5 CUPS LEMONADE

- 1 (3-inch) strip lemon zest
- 1¼ cups fresh lemon juice (about 6–10 lemons)
- ⅔ cup raw honey
- Pinch of sea salt

1 Use a vegetable peeler to remove a 3-inch strip of lemon zest. Whisk together the lemon juice, honey, and salt in a bowl until the honey is completely dissolved, which may take several minutes. Add the lemon zest to the concentrate.

2 To freeze: Because it is liquid, lemonade concentrate packs best in a rigid container. This batch will fit nicely in a 2-cup freezer container.

3 To serve: Thaw the lemonade concentrate overnight in the refrigerator, then remove the lemon zest. Combine the concentrate with 3 cups cold water, pour over ice, and serve immediately.

Variation: Honey Limeade Concentrate

Simply substitute fresh lime juice and zest in place of lemon in step 1.

Roasted Lemon-Herb Potatoes

Hands down the creamiest potatoes I've ever tasted, these are bursting with lemon flavor and are perfectly caramelized after their slow roast in the oven. I learned a version of this recipe from a friend, who learned it from a friend, who learned it from a Greek nun . . . or so the story goes.

YIELD: 6–8 SERVINGS

- 2½ pounds Yukon Gold potatoes (see Note), cut into 2-inch chunks (about 9 cups)
- ⅓ cup frozen lemon juice, thawed
- ⅓ cup water
- ⅓ cup extra-virgin olive oil
- 2 teaspoons sea salt
- ¼ teaspoon freshly ground black pepper
- 1 teaspoon dried oregano
- 1 teaspoon dried parsley
- ½ teaspoon granulated garlic
- ½ teaspoon granulated onion
- ½ teaspoon sugar

1 Preheat the oven to 400°F (200°C).

2 Place the potato chunks in a 13- by 9-inch nonreactive baking pan. Add the lemon juice, water, oil, salt, and pepper, and toss until the potatoes are evenly coated.

3 Bake for 2 to 2½ hours, stirring the potatoes every 30 minutes, until they are golden brown and starting to caramelize.

4 Evenly sprinkle the potatoes with the oregano, parsley, garlic, onion, and sugar, and toss to coat. Bake for 10 minutes longer.

NOTE: *Instead of Yukon Gold, you could substitute another all-purpose potato. I prefer to leave the skins on for this dish.*

Orange & Rosemary Mixed Nuts

Glazed with brown sugar, orange zest, and rosemary, these sweet-and-salty nuts are a favorite to have on hand around the holidays. They make a thoughtful gift and are a crowd favorite at parties. The best part? They're remarkably simple and easy to whip up!

YIELD: 3 CUPS

- 3 cups walnut or pecan halves, or a mixture of both
- 2 teaspoons frozen finely grated orange zest, thawed
- 2 tablespoons butter, melted
- 2 tablespoons dark maple syrup
- 2 tablespoons firmly packed brown sugar
- 1 tablespoon finely chopped fresh rosemary
- 1 teaspoon flaky salt

1 Preheat the oven to 350°F (180°C). Line an 18- by 13-inch baking pan with parchment paper.

2 Place the nuts in a large bowl. Combine the zest and butter in a small bowl, then pour it over the nuts. Add the maple syrup. Using a silicone spatula, fold and stir the nuts to combine.

3 Sprinkle the sugar and rosemary over the nuts, then mix until evenly coated.

4 Spread the nuts into a single layer on the prepared baking pan and then sprinkle evenly with the salt. Bake for 7 minutes. Give the nuts a good stir, making sure the nuts along the edges get moved to the middle and vice versa, then bake for 7 minutes. Stir again, then bake for 7 minutes longer, for a total of 21 minutes.

5 Allow the nuts to cool completely on the pan, then store in an airtight container.

Roasted Lemon-Herb Potatoes

Orange & Rosemary Mixed Nuts

One large fresh ear of corn yields about 1 cup of kernels.

CORN

It wouldn't feel like summer here in the Midwest without plenty of sweet corn on the cob dripping with butter! Self-serve corn stands pop up on every corner, and farmers sell fresh corn from the back of their pickup trucks in parking lots. We eat our fill and put up the rest.

Freezing Sweet Corn Kernels

While some people blanch and then place entire ears of corn in an ice bath, I find that technique cumbersome. It's much simpler to cut the kernels from the cob first, then parcook them. There's no huge pot of boiling water and no ice bath . . . I like that. I've heard of people throwing whole ears of corn, husks and all, into the freezer, but I wouldn't recommend doing so. Corn will take up much less space and will retain its flavor and nutrients longer when processed properly.

Prep. Remove the husks and silks, then stand up each ear on its flat end and cut the kernels from the cob. Find the sweet spot and don't cut too deeply—you'll know you're too deep if you feel more resistance and hear the knife cutting through the cob.

Parcook. Place the corn in a large pot and add about ¼ cup water for every 6 cups of kernels. If cooking more than 18 cups of kernels, split into multiple batches so that the kernels cook evenly. Cover and cook over medium-high heat for 10 minutes, stirring every 2 minutes and replacing the cover between stirrings. Uncover and cook for 5 minutes longer to evaporate some of the liquid. Do not use an ice bath. Spread the warm corn on a large baking pan to cool.

Freeze. Corn packs well in freezer bags or rigid containers.

Freezing Fire-Roasted Sweet Corn Kernels

You can't beat the flavor of flame-kissed corn! This can be used wherever you would use regular frozen corn but want an extra pop of char-grilled flavor. Try it in chili, black bean salsa, and corn salads.

Prep. Preheat the grill to high. The goal is to cook the corn fast and hot, just charring the outside but not overcooking it. If the grill isn't hot enough, the corn won't char and will dry out.

Remove the husks and silks, then brush each ear with extra-virgin olive oil or avocado oil, using about ½ teaspoon for every large ear. Think of the ear as a square and grill each of its four sides until the kernels turn golden brown, about 3 minutes on each side for a total of 12 minutes. Let each side fully brown before turning to the next side. Allow to cool. On a cutting board, stand each ear of corn on its flat end, and use a sharp knife to cut the kernels from the cob.

Freeze. Cool before freezing. Corn packs well in freezer bags or rigid containers.

❄ FOR THE FREEZER

Old-Fashioned Freezer Corn

Before sweet corn was bred to be tender and super sweet like it is today, folks would doll it up to make it tastier before putting it in the freezer. While sweet corn doesn't need as much sugar as it did decades ago, processing your sweet corn with a little sugar, butter, and salt means you'll have an extra-delicious side dish straight from the freezer.

YIELD: ABOUT 10 CUPS

- 10 cups raw corn kernels
- 1 cup water
- 5 tablespoons butter
- 1 tablespoon sugar
- 1½ teaspoons sea salt

1 Combine the corn, water, butter, sugar, and salt in a large pot. Bring to a boil over medium heat and simmer for about 10 minutes, stirring frequently, until the corn is just tender.

2 Spread the corn on a large baking pan to cool.

3 **To freeze:** Corn packs well in freezer bags or rigid containers. When packaging corn, make sure to evenly distribute both the corn and its liquid into each container.

Creamy Parmesan Confetti Corn

The flavors of the midsummer garden come together in this colorful side dish. Note that the vegetables are cooked together and frozen, and the cream and cheese are added when the corn is thawed and reheated. This recipe can easily be scaled up.

YIELD: 4 SERVINGS

FOR FREEZING

  1 tablespoon butter or extra-virgin olive oil

  ¼ cup diced red bell pepper

  ¼ cup diced red onion

  3 cups raw corn kernels

  ½ teaspoon sea salt

  2 tablespoons chopped fresh parsley

FOR SERVING

  ¼ cup heavy cream

  ¼ cup finely grated Parmesan cheese

1 Melt the butter in a medium saucepan over medium heat. Add the bell pepper and onion, and sauté until they start to soften, about 3 minutes.

2 Stir in the corn and salt, and cover the pan. Continue cooking, stirring occasionally and replacing the cover between stirrings, until the corn is tender, about 10 minutes. Remove the corn from the heat and stir in the parsley.

3 **To freeze:** Cool before freezing. Confetti corn packs well in freezer bags or rigid containers.

4 **To heat:** Place the thawed confetti corn in a medium saucepan and stir in the cream. Bring to a gentle simmer over medium-low heat and cook, stirring frequently, until heated through, about 5 minutes. Remove from the heat and stir in the Parmesan.

Corn Spoon Bread

Think of this as a buttery moist cornbread, so moist that it's scooped from the pan with a spoon. You could cut it into squares with a knife, but what fun would that be? I love the rustic and unique look that comes from using an ice cream scoop for serving. Pair this sweet corn cake with Mexican dishes, barbecued and grilled foods, chili, or roasted chicken.

YIELD: 8–10 SERVINGS

Cooking spray, for greasing pan

2 cups frozen corn, thawed

¾ cup water

½ cup all-purpose flour or gluten-free flour blend

½ cup finely ground cornmeal

¼ cup sugar

1 tablespoon baking powder

1 teaspoon salt

1 egg

6 tablespoons butter, melted

1 Preheat the oven to 350°F (180°C). Grease an 8-inch square baking pan.

2 Combine 1 cup of the corn with the water in a blender. Blend on high until the corn kernels are broken into smaller pieces, about 20 seconds.

3 Whisk together the flour, cornmeal, sugar, baking powder, and salt in a large bowl. Stir in the egg, butter, blended corn, and the remaining 1 cup whole corn.

4 Pour the batter into the prepared pan and bake for 50 to 55 minutes, or until golden brown around the edges. Use a spring-loaded ice cream scoop to serve. Corn spoon bread is best served warm.

CRANBERRIES

Hailing from one of the top cranberry-producing states, I have a particular fondness for these tart berries. I always stock up when they're in season so I have plenty for the entire year. They're such a nutritious and sprightly berry, and they freeze beautifully.

Freezing Whole Cranberries

Avoid the temptation to freeze cranberries in the bag they came packaged in from the store, as it is not thick enough to prevent freezer burn for very long.

Prep. Cranberries don't require any special preparation.

Freeze. Cranberries pack best in freezer bags. There is no need to flash freeze whole cranberries, as they can be easily separated when frozen together.

Cran-Raspberry Sauce

Raspberries are an exciting way to add new life to traditional cranberry sauce. Most people tend to think of this as a holiday side dish, but I like to serve it with everyday baked chicken, spoon it on yogurt, spread it on sourdough toast, or offer it on a cheese board. This sauce walks the line between tart and sweet, so feel free to increase the sugar or honey by a quarter or half cup if you'd like it on the sweeter side!

YIELD: ABOUT 4 CUPS

- 1 (12-ounce) bag cranberries (about 3 cups), fresh or frozen
- 1 cup raspberries, fresh or frozen
- ½ cup apple juice or water
- ½ cup sugar
- ½ cup honey or sugar
- ¼ teaspoon sea salt

1 Combine the cranberries, raspberries, apple juice, sugar, honey, and salt in a medium saucepan and bring to a boil. Simmer over medium heat, stirring occasionally, until the cranberries have burst open and become jammy, about 15 minutes if using fresh cranberries, 18 to 20 minutes if using frozen.

2 **To freeze:** Cool before freezing. Cranberry sauce packs well in freezer bags or rigid containers.

Variation: Traditional Cranberry Sauce

To make a more traditional cranberry sauce, follow the directions for Cran-Raspberry Sauce but use one (12-ounce) bag cranberries, 1 cup orange juice, ½ cup granulated sugar, ¼ cup firmly packed brown sugar, and ¼ teaspoon sea salt in step 1.

Cranberry-Maple Custard Pie

I first tried this pie at a small bakery in the next town over from ours, and I immediately fell in love! Creamy, sweet maple custard makes a fantastic vehicle for tart cranberries, especially when wrapped in a flaky piecrust. This has become my favorite pie to make during fall and winter, and it's a new staple on my holiday table.

YIELD: 8 SERVINGS

- 1 (9-inch) prepared piecrust
- 4 eggs
- ½ cup sugar
- 2 tablespoons all-purpose flour or gluten-free flour blend
- ½ teaspoon finely grated orange zest
- ½ teaspoon sea salt
- ¾ cup heavy cream
- ⅔ cup dark maple syrup
- 1 teaspoon vanilla extract
- 2 cups frozen cranberries

1 Chill the piecrust for 30 minutes, then preheat the oven to 400°F (200°C).

2 To blind bake the crust, lay a piece of parchment paper gently in the piecrust, then fill it to the top with pie weights, uncooked rice, or dried beans. Bake for 15 minutes, until the edges of the crust are starting to brown.

3 Carefully remove the weights and parchment paper. Prick the bottom of the crust several times with a fork, then continue baking until the bottom of the crust is starting to brown, about 15 minutes longer.

4 Beat 1 of the eggs in a small bowl. Use a pastry brush to coat the bottom and sides of the warm pie shell (not the crimped edge) with the egg wash; you should use about half the egg wash (save the rest for the filling). Allow the pie shell to cool completely, about 30 minutes.

5 Reset the oven to 325°F (160°C).

6 Whisk together the sugar, flour, orange zest, and salt in a large bowl. Whisk in the remaining egg wash, along with the 3 remaining eggs, cream, maple syrup, and vanilla.

7 Pour the filling into the pie shell, then top with the cranberries.

8 Bake for about 1 hour, or until most of the pie is set and only the very center is still jiggly. Chill completely before cutting and serving.

CUCUMBERS

Although a rather unconventional veggie to freeze, cucumbers have several uses when frozen. You can use raw frozen cucumbers to flavor sauces and sparkling water or add freshness to blended drinks. Freezer pickles are also worth making (see Intro to Freezer Pickles below). For best results, process cucumbers soon after picking. If this isn't possible, store them in the refrigerator until you can get to them.

Freezing Cucumber Slices

The flavor of raw cucumber changes slightly in the freezer, but it still tastes good. Cucumbers will be limp and release a lot of water once thawed, so they aren't the cucumber you want on your fresh garden salad.

Prep. Cut cucumbers in half lengthwise, then cut into slices that are ½ inch thick. Do not blanch.

Freeze. Flash freeze raw cucumbers, then transfer to a freezer bag for storage.

INTRO TO FREEZER PICKLES

Freezer pickles are briny and limp but still surprisingly crunchy. To make them, you simply combine cucumbers with a brine and stash them in the freezer—that's it! They're incredibly easy to make and are quite tasty.

Thickness is important for freezer pickles, because if cut too thick the texture will become off-putting; spears, halves, or whole cucumbers won't work here. Use a mandoline slicer if you have one. The acidity level of the brine is fairly specific, so I don't recommend trying to convert your favorite canning or refrigerator pickles to the freezer.

Once thawed, freezer pickles will keep in the refrigerator for up to 1 week.

Grandma's Sweet Freezer Pickles

If you like the sweet-and-sour zip of an old-fashioned bread-and-butter pickle, you'll love these. This version was adapted from my Grandma Catherine's recipe, which were the freezer pickles I grew up eating—they're my absolute favorite! Serve these with barbecue or anything grilled.

YIELD: 4 PINTS

- 2½ cups distilled white vinegar
- 2 cups sugar
- 2 cups water
- 1 tablespoon sea salt
- 2 teaspoons whole yellow mustard seed
- ¼ teaspoon celery seed
- ¼ teaspoon ground turmeric
- 8 cups sliced pickling cucumbers, ⅛–¼ inch thick (2–2½ pounds whole)
- ½ medium sweet onion, thinly sliced

1 Combine the vinegar, sugar, water, and salt in a medium saucepan over medium heat. Continuously stir just until the sugar dissolves, about 5 minutes, then remove from the heat.

2 Whisk in the mustard seed, celery seed, and turmeric. Allow the mixture to cool completely, about 1 hour.

3 Place the cucumbers and onion in a large nonreactive bowl, pour the cooled brine over them, and push them down to submerge them.

4 Cover and refrigerate overnight before eating or freezing.

5 **To freeze:** Portion the pickles into freezer containers, making sure each container has an equal amount of cucumber, onion, and brine, then freeze. Because of the brine, pickles pack best in rigid containers.

Garlic Dill Pickles

These classic dill-and-garlic pickles are ideal for piling on hamburgers and sandwiches. Because the process of freezing cucumbers accentuates the vinegar flavor, and there's no sugar in this recipe to balance the vinegar's tang, the light brine keeps the pickles from being too sour.

YIELD: 3 PINTS

> 6 cups sliced pickling cucumbers, ⅛–¼ inch thick (1½–2 pounds whole)
>
> 2 garlic cloves, thinly sliced
>
> Dill sprigs, 3 heads and 6 fronds
>
> 3 cups water
>
> ⅔ cup distilled white vinegar
>
> 1 tablespoon sea salt

1 Layer the cucumbers with the garlic and dill heads and fronds in a large nonreactive bowl.

2 In a separate bowl, whisk together the water, vinegar, and salt until the salt is dissolved, about 1 minute. Pour the brine over the cucumbers in the bowl, and push them down to submerge them.

3 Cover and refrigerate overnight before eating or freezing.

4 **To freeze:** Portion the pickles into freezer containers, making sure each container has an equal amount of cucumbers, dill, garlic, and brine, then freeze. Because of the brine, pickles pack best in rigid containers.

Half-Sweet Pickle Relish

Sweet but not too sweet, this flavorful relish is great on hot dogs or stirred into canned tuna along with a dollop of mayo for instant tuna salad. Pickle relish is cooked, which means it's naturally a good candidate for the freezer and the texture won't be affected. Store-bought relish often contains food dyes, which is why they're so brightly colored compared to this homemade version. I don't mind the bland color one bit if it means a healthier relish!

YIELD: ABOUT 2 CUPS

> 4 cups finely chopped pickling cucumbers (about 2 pounds whole; see Note)
>
> 2 teaspoons sea salt
>
> ½ cup chopped yellow onion
>
> ¼ cup chopped red bell pepper
>
> ⅓ cup sugar
>
> ¼ cup apple cider vinegar
>
> ½ teaspoon whole yellow mustard seed

1 Mix the cucumbers and salt together in a bowl and let sit for 30 minutes. Drain the cucumbers in a sieve and use the back of a spoon to gently press out more of the liquid.

2 Combine the cucumbers with the onion, bell pepper, sugar, vinegar, and mustard seed in a medium saucepan. Cook over medium heat, stirring occasionally, until most of the liquid has evaporated and the cucumbers have turned from bright green to drab yellow-green, about 20 minutes.

3 **To freeze:** Cool before freezing. Pickle relish packs well in freezer bags or rigid containers.

NOTE: *You can use a food processor to make quick work of chopping the cucumbers, but be careful not to overprocess them. If your cucumbers are overgrown or contain a large seed cavity in the center, cut the cucumbers in half lengthwise and scoop out the seeds before chopping.*

EGGPLANT

An eggplant is like a giant sponge, so it won't fare well being blanched, but it does still benefit from being heat-treated before freezing. The techniques and recipes here were developed using the most common purple globe eggplant, but they can be adapted to other varieties.

Freezing Grilled Eggplant Slices

When grilled fast and hot, eggplant will take on a delectable smoky flavor but still hold its shape. Think of grilling as a form of blanching, with the goal being to heat it quickly and to not overcook it.

Prep. Remove the stem, then cut the eggplant into round slices ¾ to 1 inch thick. Brush both sides of each slice with a thin coat of extra-virgin olive oil.

Grill. Place the slices on a very hot grill, close the lid, and cook for 4 to 5 minutes on each side. The eggplant is done when it has grill marks and is soft but not mushy.

Freeze. Cool before freezing. Eggplant slices pack best in freezer bags. Consider flash freezing to use in smaller quantities.

Freezing Roasted Eggplant

Roasting eggplant will bring out its best flavor and ensure that it keeps in the freezer a long time. Use it as a side dish or in recipes where the soft texture will disappear into the background, such as puréed dishes, dips, or pasta sauces.

Prep. Whether or not to peel the eggplant is up to you. Remove the stem and cut the eggplant into 1-inch cubes.

Cook. Pile the cubes onto a baking pan, drizzle with extra-virgin olive oil (use 1½ to 2 tablespoons oil for every large eggplant), toss to coat, then spread the eggplant into a single layer. Bake in a 425°F (220°C) oven for 30 to 40 minutes, or until they turn golden brown.

Freeze. Cool before freezing. Eggplant packs well in freezer bags or rigid containers. It can also be puréed before being frozen.

Baingan Bharta
(Spicy Eggplant Dip)

This Indian-inspired dish of fire-roasted eggplant mixed with aromatic veggies and spices has a smoky flavor and a natural creaminess from the eggplant. It's most commonly served warm with roti or paratha—two types of flatbread—although I love it spread on a grilled baguette or as a dip for tortilla chips.

YIELD: ABOUT 2 CUPS

- 1 large dark purple eggplant
- 2 tablespoons extra-virgin olive oil or avocado oil
- ½ medium red onion, finely diced
- 2 garlic cloves, grated
- 1 teaspoon grated fresh ginger
- 1 small serrano pepper, stemmed, deseeded, and finely diced
- 1 large tomato, diced
- 1 teaspoon ground coriander
- ¾ teaspoon sea salt
- 2 tablespoons chopped fresh cilantro

1 Position an oven rack in the middle of the oven and preheat the broiler.

2 Remove the stem, then cut the eggplant in half from top to bottom. Place the eggplant cut-side down on a baking pan (do not use parchment paper). Broil the eggplant until the skin is completely black and charred and the eggplant is bubbling and sizzling around the edges, 8 to 12 minutes.

3 Remove the pan from the oven and immediately cover the eggplant with a piece of aluminum foil. Allow it to steam on the pan for 10 minutes.

4 Peel and discard the charred skin from the eggplant. Use a handheld masher to mash the eggplant right on the baking pan.

5 Heat the oil in a skillet over medium heat. Add the onion and sauté until almost tender, about 5 minutes. Add the garlic, ginger, and serrano, and cook until fragrant but not browning, about 3 minutes.

6 Stir in the mashed eggplant, tomato, coriander, and salt, and continue cooking until the tomato is soft, about 8 minutes.

7 Remove from the heat and stir in the cilantro.

8 **To freeze:** Cool before freezing. Baingan bharta packs well in freezer bags or rigid containers.

9 **To heat:** Place thawed baingan bharta in a saucepan with a splash of water, cover, and cook over low heat until heated through, about 7 minutes. It can also be warmed in the microwave.

FIGS

As a cold-climate dweller, I can only dream about trees laden with figs. If you're fortunate enough to have fig trees, frozen figs are a treasure for baking, making preserves, or eating as a snack when partially thawed.

Freezing Figs

Prep. Start with ripe, soft figs and remove the stems. Figs can be frozen whole, but they'll take up less room and pack better if cut into halves or quarters.

Freeze. Figs pack best in freezer bags. Consider flash freezing figs to use in smaller quantities.

Fig & Honey Preserves

Forget the toast: These fancy preserves are begging to be served with cheese! My favorite way to eat this is spread on a seedy cracker with some aged white cheddar. A lovely floral honey pairs well with figs and enhances their complex flavor. I always have a jar of this in the freezer for adding to a cheese or charcuterie board.

YIELD: ABOUT 6 CUPS

- 12 cups ½-inch chopped figs (about 4 pounds whole)
- 2 cups sugar
- 1 cup honey
- ¼ cup lemon juice
- ¼ teaspoon sea salt

1. Chill a small ceramic or glass plate in the freezer.

2. Combine the figs, sugar, honey, lemon juice, and salt in a medium saucepan. Cook over low heat, stirring frequently, until the figs have released some of their juice, about 15 minutes.

3. Increase the heat to medium and continue cooking, stirring occasionally, until the figs have a thick, jammy appearance and reach a temperature of 220°F (104°C), about 1 hour and 20 minutes.

4. Remove the plate from the freezer and place a small spoonful of the hot fig preserves on it. Let sit for about 30 seconds, and then drag your finger through it, noting the consistency (see photo below). If the preserves are not gelled, cook for 5 to 10 minutes longer and test again with the chilled plate. Remove the pan from the heat once the preserves are set—that is, thickened to the consistency of jam.

5. **To freeze:** Cool before freezing. Because it is thick, fig preserves pack best in rigid containers.

⟐ FOR THE TABLE

Fig Cookie Smoothie

Fresh figs are abundant in fiber and minerals. A healthy way to utilize this nutrition is to toss the figs in a smoothie . . . even better if that smoothie tastes like an oatmeal cookie! The texture of this drink is light and airy yet thick, and because of all the fiber, it is incredibly satisfying.

YIELD: 1 SERVING

- 1 cup frozen fig halves
- 1 tablespoon old-fashioned oats
- 2 teaspoons almond butter
- 2 teaspoons honey or maple syrup (optional)
- 1 cup milk or nondairy alternative
- ¼ teaspoon vanilla extract
- Dash of ground cinnamon

Combine the figs, oats, almond butter, honey (if using), milk, vanilla, and cinnamon in a blender. Blend on high until smooth, about 30 seconds, then serve immediately.

GARLIC CLOVES & SCAPES

Garlic is a staple food that I use nearly every day, which means that growing our own year's supply is extra rewarding! If garlic doesn't have a long storage life in your climate, try the freezer.

Freezing Whole or Minced Garlic Cloves

Thawed garlic will be soft and have a slightly different flavor than fresh, but garlic is still worth freezing. Garlic cloves can be frozen whole, which is my preference,

or minced. Whole frozen cloves will thaw very quickly, so you don't have to plan far in advance to use them. Chopped garlic smells strong, which can stink up the freezer even when double bagged. The choice is yours.

Prep. Peel whole garlic cloves before freezing. If mincing a lot of garlic, a food processor is incredibly handy.

Freeze. Flash freeze whole garlic cloves, then transfer to a freezer container for storage. Freeze minced garlic in silicone molds with a small amount of extra-virgin olive oil or water to hold it together.

Garlic Scape Flavor Bombs

About 1 month before hardneck garlic is ready to harvest, the plant will send up a curly flower stalk called a scape. These are edible and have mild garlic flavor with a hint of onion and the snap of an asparagus spear. When I've had my fill of fresh scapes and they're still coming, I make these flavor bombs. They're easy to add to dishes such as soup, slow-cooker meals, and marinades.

YIELD: ABOUT 1 CUP

> 2 cups 1-inch garlic scape pieces
>
> ¼ cup water

1 Place the garlic scape pieces and water in a blender. Blend on high until they break down and look fibrous but creamy, about 60 seconds. Periodically stop and use a spatula to scrape down the sides of the blender as needed.

2 **To freeze:** Use a small spring-loaded scoop to portion the scape purée onto a parchment paper-lined pan and flash freeze. Garlic scape purée can also be frozen in silicone molds or ice cube trays.

Roasted Garlic Paste

Roasted garlic is one of life's great pleasures; it's mellow, nutty, and soft as butter—a marvelous transformation! Hardneck and softneck garlic varieties will both work here. You can scale up this recipe by using a larger pan; just make sure the garlic fills the pan but remains in a single layer. And by the way, your home is about to smell incredible!

YIELD: ABOUT 1 CUP

> 2 cups peeled garlic cloves
>
> 4 teaspoons extra-virgin olive oil

1 Preheat the oven to 350°F (180°C).

2 Place the garlic cloves in a 9- by 4-inch loaf pan and toss them with the oil. Cover the pan tightly with aluminum foil and bake for 90 minutes, stirring the garlic every 30 minutes and replacing the foil tightly after each stirring.

3 Allow to cool for 5 minutes, then transfer to a food processor and pulse until the garlic forms a paste. Alternatively, the garlic can be smashed in the pan with the back of a spoon, although the paste won't be quite as smooth.

4 **To freeze:** Use a small spring-loaded scoop to portion the garlic paste onto a parchment paper-lined pan and flash freeze. Garlic paste can also be frozen in silicone molds or ice cube trays.

GINGER & TURMERIC

If you're fortunate enough to have a bumper crop of either of these earthy medicinal roots (or you find a sale at the grocery store), freezing is a choice way to preserve them. That punch-you-in-the-nose scent of fresh ginger just can't be beat, and the bright orange-yellow color of turmeric lets you know that it packs a lot of potency! Frozen ginger and turmeric can be used for cooking and making tea.

Freezing Ginger & Turmeric Chunks

I prefer to freeze ginger and turmeric in chunks, rather than grate them or cut them into slices before freezing, because I find that they keep their potency better. They can be grated on a rasp grater while still frozen or cut into slices once thawed.

Prep. Cut ginger and turmeric into approximately 1-inch sections. There is no need to peel the roots first.

Freeze. Flash freeze the root pieces, then transfer to a freezer container for storage. Ginger and turmeric freeze well in bags or rigid containers.

GRAPES

I remember the first time I stumbled upon wild grapes draping through the tree canopy like something out of a medieval painting. They made some of the best grape juice and jelly I've ever had! Grapes are a fun and often overlooked fruit for the freezer. Sweet table grapes without seeds can be frozen whole, and seedy grapes are well suited for making juice that can be frozen for drinking or transformed into jelly or freezer pops.

Freezing Whole Grapes

Like miniature ice pop spheres, frozen seedless grapes are a cooling treat during warm months and make a unique addition to smoothies.

Prep. Remove the grapes from their stems. If the grapes have seeds, you can cut each grape in half lengthwise and pick out the seeds, although this is a bit labor intensive—I prefer to turn seeded grapes into juice.

Freeze. Grapes pack best in freezer bags. There is no need to flash freeze whole grapes, as they can be easily separated when frozen together. Halved grapes will stick together and should be flash frozen.

Making and Freezing Grape Juice

Grapes can be juiced using a juicer, although you'll want to exercise caution with seeded grapes, because grinding the seeds with the flesh can make the juice bitter. My preferred method for juicing grapes is to use heat.

Prep. Wash and destem the grapes, then place them in a large pot. Add ½ cup water for every 5 pounds of grapes. Cook over medium heat, using a handheld masher to crush the grapes and get their juices flowing. Simmer, stirring frequently, until the grape flesh dissolves and the seeds are released, 15 to 20 minutes. If working through a lot of grapes, process them in batches.

Set a fine-mesh sieve over a large bowl. Ladle the grape mixture into the sieve and allow it to strain for 1 to 2 hours, stirring ocassionally. You can also use cheesecloth or a jelly bag. For a large quantity of grapes, consider using a food mill.

Freeze. Cool before freezing. Because it is liquid, grape juice packs best in rigid containers. Smaller portions can be frozen in a silicone mold.

🍴 FOR THE TABLE

Mulled Grape Cider

This is the drink I want warming my hands on a cool fall evening in front of a bonfire. The spice is subtle, and the combination of grape and apple is enchanting. Make your own mulling spice blend or use a premade store-bought mix—just make sure it contains orange peel, cinnamon, cloves, and allspice.

YIELD: 4 SERVINGS

- 3 cups frozen grape juice, thawed
- 1 cup apple cider
- 2 tablespoons mulling spices
- 4 cinnamon sticks, for serving (optional)

1 Combine the grape juice and apple cider in a medium saucepan over medium heat.

2 Place the mulling spices in a tea ball or tea bag, then submerge it in the juice. Alternatively, place the mulling spices directly in the juice, then strain through a fine-mesh strainer before serving.

3 Bring to a boil and simmer gently for 10 minutes. Remove the mulling spices and serve hot. Garnish each mug with a cinnamon stick, if using.

🍴 FOR THE TABLE

Grape Lassi

A lassi is a popular yogurt-based beverage from northern India that drinks like a thin milkshake. This recipe is reminiscent of my favorite childhood treat from the local ice cream shop, which was part tangy grape slushie and part sweet vanilla soft serve ice cream.

YIELD: 1 SERVING

- 1 cup frozen purple grapes
- ¼ cup plain Greek yogurt
- ½ cup milk or nondairy alternative
- 1 teaspoon honey or sugar (optional)

Combine the grapes, yogurt, milk, and honey, if using, in a blender. Blend on high until smooth, about 30 seconds, and serve immediately.

GREEN BEANS

I have many childhood memories of my mom sitting on the couch with a towel spread across her lap and a bag of green beans at her side. *Snap! Snap! Snap!* I've been eating homegrown frozen green beans since I was a child, and now they're a staple in my garden and in my freezer as well. The variety of green bean can make a big difference; some aren't well suited for freezing, such as yellow wax beans, most large flat beans, and even some green varieties. Some freezer-friendly varieties to try are Top Crop, Contender, and Jade.

Perfectly Crunchy Beans Every Time!

Have you been disappointed by mushy frozen green beans? Try this steam-blanching method for crunchy, squeaky green beans!

Freezing Whole and Cut Green Beans

Join in any discussion with passionate food preservers and you'll hear an impressive list of different ways to freeze green beans. Many people swear by freezing them raw without blanching. Yes, this is a time-saver, but I've tried it and find the taste and texture to be quite unpleasant.

Prep. Green beans can be frozen whole or snapped into smaller pieces. Start by destemming them, and, if desired, snap them into bite-size pieces.

Blanch. Steam blanch (see page 10) for 3 minutes, tossing the beans around at the 90-second mark. Move immediately to an ice bath and chill for 3 minutes. Drain as much water from the beans as possible, then transfer to a towel-lined pan to dry.

Freeze. Green beans pack best in freezer bags.

Heat. The secret to preparing frozen green beans is to not overcook them. For simple green beans, put 1 tablespoon water in a medium saucepan along with the thawed green beans, cover, and cook over medium heat for 3 to 5 minutes, or until the beans are just tender.

🍴 **FOR THE TABLE**

Garlic-Sesame Green Beans

A little spicy and packed with umami flavor, these beans make a great side dish for all of my favorite Asian-inspired entrées—from sweet-and-sour chicken to lo mein or pot stickers.

YIELD: 4 SERVINGS

- 1 tablespoon toasted sesame oil
- 1 quart frozen green beans (about 4 cups), thawed
- 2 garlic cloves, minced
- 1 tablespoon soy sauce
- 2 teaspoons honey
- ¼ teaspoon crushed red pepper
- ¼ teaspoon fish sauce (optional)
- 1 teaspoon sesame seeds

1 Heat the oil in a skillet over medium heat. Add the green beans and sauté until almost tender, about 3 minutes.

2 Move the beans to the sides of the pan, creating a bare spot in the center. Add the garlic, soy sauce, honey, crushed red pepper, and fish sauce, if using, in the center of the pan. Cook for 1 minute, then toss the beans around and sauté until tender, about 2 minutes longer.

3 Top with the sesame seeds and serve.

One frozen puck of greens equals about 2 cups of chopped fresh.

GREENS

Greens such as lettuce, kale, chard, collards, and spinach can be plentiful in the garden, and freezing is easily the best way to preserve them. Dark leafy greens are one of my favorite freezer staples, and believe it or not, lettuce can be frozen too!

Freezing Dark Leafy Green "Pucks"

This method works on any dark leafy green, such as kale, spinach, and Swiss chard—or even beet and dandelion greens. Frozen greens will be wilted once thawed, so they won't work for fresh salads, but they are perfect for anything cooked.

Prep. If the leaves have a fibrous center stem, tear the tender leafy part of the greens from it. Cut or tear the leaves into large bite-size pieces.

Blanch. Steam blanch (see page 10) for 3 minutes, using tongs to toss the greens around at the 90-second mark. Work in batches, and do not overcrowd the pot. About two large handfuls is a good amount for a standard large steamer pot. Do not use an ice bath.

Transfer the greens to a baking pan. While the greens are still warm, pack them into a silicone muffin pan—really stuff them in there! You can also use a metal muffin pan, but you will need to set the pan in warm water to loosen and remove the frozen pucks.

Freeze. Allow the greens to cool before freezing. Place the pan in the freezer until the greens are completely frozen, then pop out the pucks and transfer to a freezer bag for storage.

Frozen lettuce

Freezing Lettuce

Freezing lettuce is a good solution if you have a lot of it that needs to be used up quickly, such as when it's threatening to flower and go to seed. Frozen lettuce can be used in a green juice or blended into a smoothie. It has a pleasantly grassy taste, which can be prominent or virtually undetectable depending on how much you add to a dish and what other flavors you blend with it.

Prep. There's no need to dry your lettuce after washing. Pack the lettuce into a blender, and blend on high until smooth, about 30 seconds. Stop to scrape down the sides as needed, and if your blender has a plunger, use it to push down the lettuce. Add a small amount of water if the machine needs help blending.

Freeze. Pour the puréed lettuce into silicone molds or ice cube trays, and place in the freezer until completely frozen. I use the smallest mold that I have for this (about 2 to 3 teaspoons' worth), as blended lettuce is very concentrated. If you have only larger molds, don't fill them all the way.

Garlic-Butter Kale

I can't think of a better way to eat kale than drenched in garlic butter! When harvested in cool weather and preserved properly, frozen kale is sweet and tender and stands on its own as a side dish. Although this recipe calls for kale, you can substitute any dark leafy green.

YIELD: 3–4 SERVINGS

   2 tablespoons butter

   1 garlic clove, minced

   3 frozen kale pucks (page 105), thawed

   ⅛ teaspoon sea salt

1 Melt the butter in a skillet over medium heat. Add the garlic and sauté until it is fragrant but not browned, about 1 minute.

2 Stir in the kale and salt. Cook, stirring frequently, until the greens are tender, about 5 minutes.

Cheeseburger Soup

This is the number one favorite soup in our household. It's a simple and hearty soup with no frills and nothing fancy, made with pantry, fridge, and freezer staples you likely have on hand. And it's always a winner! If you don't eat dairy, make "hamburger soup" instead by adding a 15-ounce can of diced tomatoes in step 3 and omitting the cheese—it will still be excellent.

YIELD: 6 SERVINGS

- 2 tablespoons extra-virgin olive oil, avocado oil, or lard
- 2 pounds lean ground beef
- 1 medium yellow onion, diced
- 3 celery stalks, diced
- 4 cups chicken broth
- 2 large carrots, diced
- 2 cups diced potatoes
- 2 garlic cloves, minced
- 2 teaspoons dried basil
- 1 teaspoon dried oregano
- ¼ teaspoon freshly ground black pepper
- 1-2 frozen spinach or Swiss chard pucks (page 105), thawed
- 8 ounces medium cheddar cheese, shredded

  Sea salt

1 Heat 1 tablespoon of the oil in a skillet over medium heat. Add the beef and cook, stirring and chopping it into small pieces, until browned, about 10 minutes. Drain any excess fat, and set the meat aside.

2 Heat the remaining 1 tablespoon oil in a large pot over medium heat. Add the onion and celery, and sauté until tender, about 7 minutes.

3 Add the broth, carrots, potatoes, garlic, basil, oregano, and pepper, and stir in the beef. Simmer until the potatoes and carrots are tender, about 15 minutes.

4 Roughly chop the spinach to break it into smaller pieces, then add it to the soup. Stir in the cheese and cook for 3 minutes.

5 Because some broths are saltier than others, taste the soup and add salt if necessary. I typically add about 1 teaspoon salt.

HERBS

If I had only a small space to garden, I'd prioritize growing herbs. I use them every day during the growing season, and they make meals come to life. I always grow enough to use fresh, plus plenty for putting up!

Freezing Basil

Basil: the quintessential smell of summer! And it's the only common herb that benefits from a slightly different freezing technique than the others. Coating the leaves in a thin layer of olive oil helps prevent freezer burn and makes it easier to break off a chunk when needed. The flavor of frozen basil is similar to fresh, but the leaves will darken and wilt, so frozen basil is best suited for cooking.

Prep. Basil bruises easily, so be very gentle when working with it. Start with clean, dry basil, and pluck the leaves from the stems. Measure the leaves and place them in a large bowl. For every 3 packed cups of fresh basil, drizzle over 1 tablespoon extra-virgin olive oil. Gently toss and fluff the leaves until they are all evenly coated with the oil.

Freeze. Pack the oiled basil leaves into quart freezer bags, gently pressing the basil together into one big mass, then freeze immediately. Up to 6 cups of basil will fit in a quart bag. If working with a larger amount, use multiple quart bags instead of increasing to a gallon bag. To use, simply break off a section of basil whenever you need some—no need to let it thaw.

Basil frozen with a light coating of olive oil

Freezing Other Herbs

There's a common practice of preserving herbs by chopping and freezing them in an ice cube tray filled with olive oil. This method works fine, but it's impractical for the way I cook. I like to use a lot of herbs, and I don't want to use that much oil along with them.

The good news is that most herbs freeze well without oil. I simply chop the herbs, stuff them into a container, and freeze—that's it! The following herbs freeze well with this technique:

- Chives
- Cilantro
- Dill

- Marjoram
- Mint
- Oregano
- Parsley

- Rosemary
- Thyme
- Sage

Once thawed, frozen herbs will be darker and have a translucent quality. They are best suited for use in cooking, not for using as a fresh garnish.

FREEZING DILL FOR PICKLES

Have you ever run into the problem of having cucumbers ready for pickling but no fresh dill to go with them? Timing dill and cukes to be ready at the same time can be a challenge, with dill often drying up before the cucumbers are ready.

Whole dill heads and fronds can be frozen and thawed later for pickle making. Frozen dill has slightly less flavor than fresh, but much more flavor than dried.

Dill doesn't require any special preparation. Just pack whole dill heads and fronds into freezer bags and freeze.

Prep. Herbs freeze best when completely dry, so if you choose to wash them, make sure to dry them really well. Strip the leafy part of the herb from the stalks or stems, and mince the leaves. Herbs chopped by hand with a sharp knife will yield the best product; a food processor will tear them up and the quality will be lower.

Freeze. Herbs pack well in freezer bags or rigid containers. If the herbs are fully dry, they won't stick together, and you will be able to pinch them, still frozen, right out of the container. If the herbs are moist, they will stick together, and storing them in a freezer bag will make it easier to break off a chunk. It's better to use several small containers rather than one big container; an 8-ounce container or a quart freezer bag is a good size.

Special thawing instructions. Frozen herbs start to thaw instantly, so take out the container, remove what you need, and put the container back in the freezer immediately.

Winter Soup Herb Blend

FROZEN HERB BLENDS

A big stash of different frozen herb blends is equally handy and delicious! Follow the directions for freezing herbs, taking care that your blends are well mixed before portioning them into containers. The parts below are measured in volume. I usually use a ¼ cup measure as my "part."

Winter Soup Herb Blend

When I have a pot of soup bubbling away on the stove, you can bet the soup will include this herb blend! This is my essential savory blend for meat, potatoes, and everything in between.

- 5 parts minced fresh parsley
- 2 parts minced fresh sage
- 2 parts minced fresh thyme
- 1 part minced fresh rosemary

Ranch Herb Blend

Keeping this blend on hand means herby ranch vegetable dip or dressing anytime. Try this seasoning on chicken, meatloaf, or roasted potatoes.

- 8 parts minced fresh parsley
- 4 parts minced fresh chives
- 1 part minced fresh dill

Greek Herb Blend

This is my go-to for anything Greek, from chicken gyros to flavorful meatballs. Try it on chicken and lamb.

- 8 parts minced fresh parsley
- 4 parts minced fresh oregano
- 1 part minced fresh dill
- 1 part minced fresh mint
- 1 part minced fresh rosemary
- 1 part minced fresh thyme

Basil Pesto

I'm particular about my basil pesto—I want it to be heavy on basil flavor, not overpowered by garlic, and marvelously nutty from the Parmesan and walnuts. The olive oil is a major component, so use the good stuff! Of course, we combine homemade pesto with pasta, but it's also wonderful stirred into soups, added to meatballs, slathered on chicken breast, and scrambled into eggs.

YIELD: ABOUT 1½ CUPS

- ½ cup coarsely grated Parmesan cheese
- ½ cup raw walnut halves
- 1 tablespoon minced fresh garlic
- 2 cups very firmly packed fresh basil leaves (see Note)
- 2 teaspoons fresh lemon juice
- ½ teaspoon sea salt
- ⅓–½ cup extra-virgin olive oil

1 Prepare your freezer containers first, so that once the pesto is made it can be frozen immediately to prevent browning.

2 Combine the Parmesan, walnuts, and garlic in a food processor. Pulse 10 to 15 times, until the mixture is crumbly.

3 Add the basil, lemon juice, and salt. Process until the mixture is finely ground, about 30 seconds. Stop to scrape down the sides of the bowl as necessary.

4 With the machine running, slowly stream in the oil, starting with ⅓ cup. If the pesto sticks to the sides of the bowl, stop to scrape it down, then continue. If your pesto is dry, add up to 2 tablespoons more oil until it comes together and flows freely in the bowl. Process for 30 seconds longer to make sure the pesto is well combined.

5 **To freeze:** Freeze immediately. Pesto packs best in rigid containers. Consider freezing smaller portions in a silicone mold.

6 **To thaw:** Avoid heat when thawing pesto, and thaw only what you'll use within 1 or 2 days.

NOTE: *It's important that the basil be very firmly packed in the measuring cup. Hold it down with one hand in the cup while you keep stuffing in more!*

Pesto Vegetable Minestrone

Brimming with veggies, beans, and noodles, this light yet substantial soup is packed with fiber and is notably filling. A scoop of pesto is a wonderful complement to the tomatoey broth.

YIELD: 6–8 SERVINGS

- 1 tablespoon extra-virgin olive oil, avocado oil, or lard
- 3 celery stalks, diced
- 1 medium yellow onion, diced
- 2 medium carrots, diced
- 2 garlic cloves, minced
- 1 teaspoon dried basil
- 1 teaspoon dried oregano
- ½ teaspoon dried thyme
- 6 cups chicken or vegetable broth
- 1 (14.5-ounce) can diced tomatoes
- 2 tablespoons tomato paste
- 2 cups diced zucchini (about 1 medium)
- 1 (15-ounce) can Great Northern beans, drained and rinsed
- 1 (15-ounce) can kidney beans, drained and rinsed
  Sea salt
- 2 cups cooked elbow macaroni (1 heaping cup dry)
- 3 tablespoons frozen basil pesto (page 111), thawed
  Grated Parmesan cheese, for serving

1 Heat the oil in a large pot over medium heat. Add the celery and onion, and sauté, stirring occasionally, until tender, about 7 minutes.

2 Add the carrots, garlic, basil, oregano, thyme, broth, diced tomatoes, and tomato paste. Bring to a boil, then simmer gently for 15 minutes.

3 Stir in the zucchini and beans, and return to a simmer. Cook until the zucchini is tender, about 10 minutes.

4 Because some broths are saltier than others, taste the soup and add salt if necessary. I typically add about 1 teaspoon salt.

5 Remove from the heat and stir in the macaroni and pesto. Ladle into bowls and top with a sprinkle of Parmesan.

Ranch Veggie Dip

A vegetable dip is a foolproof way to get me to eat more vegetables, especially when the dip is made with (frozen) fresh herbs! I like an ultracreamy ranch dip with tons of herby flavor, and this one hits all the marks. To turn this dip into dressing, simply thin to your desired consistency with about ¼ cup milk, buttermilk, or water.

YIELD: 1 CUP

- ½ cup sour cream
- ¼ cup mayonnaise
- 2 tablespoons frozen Ranch Herb Blend (page 110)
- 1 teaspoon lemon juice
- ½ teaspoon granulated onion
- ½ teaspoon granulated garlic
- ¼ teaspoon sea salt

1 Whisk together the sour cream, mayonnaise, herb blend, lemon juice, onion, garlic, and salt in a bowl.

2 Refrigerate for 1 hour before serving, if possible, to allow the flavors to meld.

Greek Meatballs

Like a gyro in meatball form, these are reminiscent of the authentic gyros served at the Greek restaurant I've been eating at since I was a kid. They're moist, tender, and full of big flavor from the garlic, onion, and herbs. I serve these with fries baked in olive oil (page 150) and a hearty helping of homemade tzatziki sauce.

YIELD: 5–6 SERVINGS

- 1 slice sandwich bread, any type
- ¼ cup milk or water
- 1 egg
- ½ small red or yellow onion, finely chopped
- 3 tablespoons frozen Greek Herb Blend (page 110)
- 2 garlic cloves, minced
- 1 teaspoon sea salt
- ¼ teaspoon freshly ground black pepper
- 2 pounds ground lamb or lean ground beef, or a mixture of both
- 1 tablespoon extra-virgin olive oil, avocado oil, or melted lard

1 Preheat the oven to 400°F (200°C).

2 Tear the bread into small pieces and place them in a large bowl. Pour the milk over the bread and allow it to sit and hydrate for 5 minutes.

3 Add the egg, onion, herb blend, garlic, salt, and pepper to the bread mixture and stir to create a slurry.

4 Add in the ground meat, using a fork to mix until well combined.

5 Form the mixture into balls of about 2 tablespoons each, rolling them between your palms. Work with light hands and take care not to overwork or compact the meatballs to ensure they stay tender.

6 Grease an 8-inch cast-iron skillet or 9-inch square baking pan with the oil. Place the meatballs in the pan so that they are just touching.

7 Bake for 35 to 40 minutes, or until the meatballs are cooked through and no longer pink in the center.

MANGO

Mango is one of the most popular fruits in the world for good reason—there's nothing better than a juicy, aromatic, fresh mango. Don't rely on skin color to tell if a mango is ripe. Instead, treat it like a peach or avocado and give it a gentle squeeze; a ripe mango will be slightly soft.

Freezing Mango Pieces

Prep. Mangoes should be peeled and the large central seed removed before freezing. Use a vegetable peeler to remove the skin, then cut slabs of mango flesh away from the seed. Be careful when cutting because the flesh will be slippery, but it's the best way I've found to get the most flesh. Cut the mango into 1-inch pieces. Mango purée can also be frozen.

Freeze. Mango pieces pack best in freezer bags, and purée packs well in freezer bags or rigid containers. Consider flash freezing mango pieces to use in smaller quantities.

Mango Chutney

Some chutneys lean toward being lightly cooked and fresher, and some are more jammy. This recipe is the latter; it freezes better that way. Chutney eats like a sweet-and-savory jam, full of spice and packed with mango flavor. Slather it on Indian food, grilled meats, or anything deep-fried. I adore it on a cracker with cream cheese or a strong white cheddar.

YIELD: ABOUT 2 CUPS

1 tablespoon avocado oil or other neutral oil

½ cup finely diced yellow onion

3 cups diced mango (about 3 large whole)

⅔ cup sugar

⅓ cup water

⅓ cup distilled white vinegar

1 garlic clove, grated

1 teaspoon grated fresh ginger

½ teaspoon crushed red pepper

½ teaspoon ground coriander

½ teaspoon whole yellow mustard seed

½ teaspoon sea salt

Pinch of ground cinnamon

1 Heat the oil in a medium saucepan over medium heat. Add the onion and sauté until almost tender, about 5 minutes.

2 Stir in the mango, sugar, water, vinegar, garlic, ginger, crushed red pepper, coriander, mustard seed, salt, and cinnamon, then bring to a boil. Simmer gently until the mango is tender, about 15 minutes. Use a handheld masher to crush the mango into smaller pieces.

3 Continue cooking, stirring occasionally, until the chutney has thickened to a jamlike consistency, about 22 minutes longer.

4 **To freeze:** Cool before freezing. Because it is thick, mango chutney packs best in rigid containers.

Mango Golden Milk Smoothie

Golden milk is a warm beverage made from sweetened milk and turmeric, giving the drink its signature sunny yellow color. This chilled version has all the same charming flavors, and adding frozen mango makes it even creamier and more refreshing.

YIELD: 1 SERVING

- 1 cup frozen mango pieces
- 1 cup milk or nondairy alternative
- 1 tablespoon maple syrup (optional)
- 1 teaspoon grated fresh turmeric
- ¼ teaspoon vanilla extract
- ⅛ teaspoon ground cinnamon
- ⅛ teaspoon ground ginger
- Pinch of ground cardamom
- Pinch of freshly ground black pepper

Combine the mango, milk, maple syrup (if using), turmeric, vanilla, cinnamon, ginger, cardamom, and pepper in a blender. Blend on high until smooth, about 30 seconds, and serve immediately.

MELONS

Nothing says picnics, barbecues, and summer sun quite like a juicy melon! As long as it's sweet and ripe, any type of melon can be frozen, including watermelon, honeydew, and cantaloupe. Get creative—melon is a wonderful fruit for blending with other flavors and transforming into frozen treats such as freezer pops.

Freezing Melon Pieces

Cantaloupe, honeydew, and seedless watermelon all freeze well, although they won't have the same texture as fresh. Melon makes a unique addition to smoothies and slushies, or it can be eaten partially thawed. Watermelon with seeds can be juiced, and the juice can be frozen, turned into frozen treats, or used for drinks and cocktails.

Prep. Cut the melon in half. If it has seeds and stringy bits in the center (like a cantaloupe or honeydew), use a spoon to scoop them out. Set the melon halves cut-side down on a cutting board. Use a sharp knife to pare the hard outer rind off, taking care to remove all of the bland, lighter-colored flesh underneath the rind. Cut the melon into approximately 1-inch pieces. For juice, blend seeded watermelon pieces on low speed (so as not to crush the seeds), then strain through a mesh strainer to remove the seeds.

Freeze. Flash freeze the melon, then transfer to a freezer bag for storage. Watermelon juice will freeze best in a rigid container.

Watermelon Mojito Slushies

Watermelon, strawberry, lime, and fresh mint come together to create this patio-sitting, poolside-lounging, beach-going cocktail (the rum is optional). This recipe will easily scale up if you're quenching the thirst of a larger crowd.

YIELD: 2 SERVINGS

- 3 cups frozen seedless watermelon cubes
- ½ cup frozen whole strawberries
- ⅓ cup white rum or water
- ¼ teaspoon finely grated lime zest
- ¼ cup fresh lime juice
- 3 tablespoons honey or agave syrup
- 8 fresh mint leaves
- Pinch of sea salt

Combine the watermelon, strawberries, rum, lime zest and juice, honey, mint, and salt in a blender. Blend on high until smooth, about 30 seconds, and serve immediately.

Cantaloupe & Yogurt Freezer Pops

As a child of the 80s, I spent the hottest days of summer playing outside on the Slip 'N Slide and eating freezer pops (or "freezies," as we called them). This is a much healthier version, but it is just as much fun! You can buy fillable ice pop bags online and at specialty kitchen stores.

YIELD: 5 OR 6 FREEZER POPS

- 4 cups cubed cantaloupe (about ½ large)
- ½ cup plain Greek yogurt
- 2 tablespoons honey (optional)
- ½ teaspoon vanilla extract

1 Combine the cantaloupe, yogurt, honey (if using), and vanilla in a blender. Blend on high until smooth, about 30 seconds. The purée will appear grainy or almost separated, but that will resolve once frozen.

2 **To freeze:** Pour the purée into freezer pop bags, seal, and freeze.

MUSHROOMS

Mushrooms are one of my favorite crops to grow because they make use of the shady parts of the yard where fruits and veggies won't thrive. Plus, mushrooms are incredibly rewarding to harvest (and forage!). While you can't beat a fresh mushroom fried crisp in butter, most edible mushrooms can be frozen with good success.

Freezing Sliced Mushrooms

Mushrooms should be cooked before freezing. Add thawed mushrooms directly to dishes such as soups and casseroles. Thawed mushrooms will be limp, but they can be crisped up in a skillet before adding to stir-fries or side dishes.

Prep. Cut mushrooms into slices or bite-size pieces. Sauté mushrooms in butter or extra-virgin olive oil over medium heat until they are tender and just starting to brown. Transfer the mushrooms to a baking pan to cool.

Freeze. Mushrooms pack well in freezer bags or rigid containers.

Heat. To crisp the mushrooms, reheat in a skillet with a small amount of butter or extra-virgin olive oil.

OKRA

Okra is a unique-looking vegetable in the garden, and its flowers are stunning. The pods are best when they're young and tender, about 4 inches long. They grow very fast after flowering, so don't let them get away from you!

Freezing Okra Pods

Okra will be soft once thawed, so use it in soups, stews, or gumbos. It can also be coated in flour and frozen prepped-and-ready for deep-frying.

Prep. Cut off the top of the okra stem, taking care to leave the base of the stem intact and not to expose the seeds inside.

Blanch. Steam blanch (see page 10) small pods for 4 minutes and large ones for 5 minutes, tossing the okra around at the halfway mark. Alternatively, blanch small okra pods for 3 minutes and large pods for 4 minutes in boiling water (see page 12). Move immediately to an ice bath and chill for 3 minutes. Drain as much water from the okra as possible, then transfer to a towel-lined pan to dry.

Okra can also be frozen ready for deep-frying. Follow the directions above for blanching and drying. After the okra has cooled, cut it into 1-inch pieces and toss it with flour.

Freeze. Okra packs best in freezer bags. Consider flash freezing okra to use in smaller quantities. Flash freeze flour-coated okra for deep-frying, then transfer to a freezer bag for storage.

ONIONS

A can't-live-without veggie on our homestead, onions are the base for nearly every good meal. Needless to say, we always keep plenty on hand. If your climate is not conducive to storing onions long term at room temperature, they can be frozen in many different ways.

Freezing Raw Diced Onions

Once thawed, frozen raw onions will be soft and have a slightly different smell and taste than fresh, so they're best suited for dishes that are cooked. Any variety of onion can be frozen.

Prep. Peel and dice the onions. There is no need to flash freeze diced onions, as they can be separated when frozen together in a bag.

Freeze. Onions pack best in freezer bags.

Special thawing instructions. Use frozen diced onions straight from the freezer, and don't thaw them ahead unless you have to.

Freezing Roasted Onion Slices

Onions aren't a good candidate for being blanched in boiling water, but they do benefit from being heat-treated before freezing. The easiest way to accomplish this is by roasting them. The rings of onions stay together and are easy to grab out of the freezer. Similar to frozen raw onions, these work best for cooked dishes.

Prep. Preheat the oven to 400°F (200°C). Peel the onions and cut them into slices about ½ inch thick, keeping the rings together.

Roast. Arrange the slices in a single layer on a parchment paper–lined baking pan and brush the tops very lightly with extra-virgin olive oil or avocado oil. Bake for about 30 minutes, or until the onions have just softened and are starting to brown.

Freeze. Flash freeze onion slices, then transfer to a freezer bag for storage.

Caramelized Fried Onions

Having caramelized onions in the freezer is like having culinary gold. As the onions are already soft, freezing doesn't affect their texture. Truly caramelized onions require a long, slow cook, which brings out their sweetness. My favorite preparation is a hybrid of caramelization and frying. The onions are soft and sweet but have that robust fried onion flavor—it's the best of both worlds!

YIELD: ABOUT 1 CUP

- 2 large onions, any variety
- 3 tablespoons butter, extra-virgin olive oil, or lard
- ½ teaspoon sea salt

1 Peel the onions, then cut each one into quarters. Cut into slices about ¼ inch thick.

2 Melt the butter in a skillet over low heat. Add the onions and give them a stir to coat them in the butter.

3 Cook, stirring every few minutes, until the onions have softened and turned translucent, about 20 minutes.

4 Sprinkle the onions with the salt and increase the heat to medium-high. Continue cooking, stirring frequently, until they are golden brown, about 10 minutes longer.

5 To freeze: Cool before freezing. Caramelized fried onions pack well in freezer bags or rigid containers. Consider freezing smaller portions in a silicone mold, or drop blobs of onions onto a parchment paper–lined pan and flash freeze. Transfer to a freezer bag for storage.

Pickled Red Onions

Pickled onions might seem complicated or like something you only find at a restaurant, but this vibrant pink and oh-so-tangy condiment couldn't be easier to make. Pickling softens the onions and mellows their flavor. Try pickled onions wherever you want a pop of vinegar, such as in salads or sandwiches, or on avocado toast or fish tacos.

YIELD: 3–4 CUPS

- 1 cup water
- ½ cup distilled white vinegar
- ½ cup apple cider vinegar
- ¼ cup sugar
- 1 teaspoon sea salt
- 1 large red onion, sliced ⅛ inch thick

1 Whisk together the water, vinegars, sugar, and salt in a small saucepan over medium heat until the sugar dissolves. The brine should be warm, but not boiling.

2 Place the onion slices in a medium, nonreactive bowl and pour the warm brine over the top of them. Refrigerate overnight to allow the onion to pickle.

3 **To freeze:** Portion the onion, along with its brine, into freezer containers and freeze. Because of the brine, pickled onions pack best in rigid containers.

French Onion & Cheddar Burgers

Buttery caramelized onions and melty cheddar are a great team, and together they're exceptional on top of burgers. Whether panfried or grilled, these are the burgers I find myself making over and over again—they're that good!

YIELD: 4 SERVINGS

1 pound 85% lean ground beef

1 teaspoon sea salt

⅛ teaspoon freshly ground black pepper

1 tablespoon butter or extra-virgin olive oil

4 slices medium cheddar cheese

½ cup frozen caramelized fried onions (page 123), thawed

4 hamburger buns (optional)

1 Form the beef into four equal-size patties about 1 inch thick. Season both sides evenly with the salt and pepper.

2 Melt the butter in a large cast-iron skillet (or other ovenproof skillet) over medium-high heat. Add the burger patties and cook on one side until browned, about 7 minutes. Flip and cook on the second side until they are just cooked through, about 5 minutes longer.

3 Position an oven rack in the middle of the oven and preheat the broiler.

4 Top each burger with 1 slice of the cheese, and then spread 2 tablespoons of the caramelized onions in an even layer on top of the cheese.

5 Place the skillet in the oven under the broiler, and broil the burgers until the cheese is melted and starting to bubble, about 3 minutes.

6 Use a spatula to transfer each burger to a bun, if desired, or eat them as is with a knife and fork.

PEACHES

When I'm buying peaches to preserve, I always look for freestone types because the pit comes out easily when the peach is cut in half. Clingstone peaches have pits that hold on tightly to the peach flesh. These can also be processed, but the slices won't be quite as clean-cut and beautiful because you'll have to trim around the pit.

Freezing Peach Slices

To peel or not to peel? Once thawed, peach skins will be slightly tough, which I don't prefer in things such as baked dishes but don't notice in a smoothie. Because of this, I typically remove the skins so that my frozen peaches have the most versatility.

Prep. To peel peaches, bring a large pot of water to a boil. Make a small X with a sharp paring knife in the bottom of each peach. Underripe peaches don't peel easily, so make sure you're working with ripe, juicy ones! Place no more than three peaches at a time in the boiling water and cook for 30 to 60 seconds. Watch for the skin on the bottom of the peaches to start peeling away.

Remove the peaches from the boiling water and allow them to cool slightly, but peel them while they're still warm. The peels should come off easily; if they don't, try boiling the peaches up to 1 minute longer.

Cut peeled or unpeeled peaches into slices. I prefer to freeze peaches in slices, but they can be frozen in halves, quarters, or chunks as well.

Freeze. Peaches pack best in freezer bags. Consider flash freezing peaches to use in smaller quantities. Because peaches will brown when exposed to air, work in batches and get them into the freezer as soon as they are ready.

To easily peel peaches, cut an X into the bottom, then submerge in boiling water until the skin starts to peel off, 30 to 60 seconds.

Roasted
Peach Jam

Sweet Bourbon
Baked Peaches

Roasted Peach Jam

I love taking beautiful ripe fruit, bringing out all its best characteristics, and capturing them in a jar. Roasting the peaches instead of boiling them gives this jam a lovely caramelized flavor. It's an easy jam to make because most of the work is hands-off, and there's no pectin needed.

YIELD: ABOUT 4 CUPS

- 10 cups peeled and chopped peaches (about 5 pounds whole; see Note)
- 3 cups sugar
- 2 tablespoons lemon juice
- ½ teaspoon sea salt

1 Preheat the oven to 350°F (180°C).

2 Combine the peaches, sugar, lemon juice, and salt in a large pot over medium heat.

3 Bring to a boil, then use a handheld masher to break the peaches into smaller pieces while they heat. Boil for about 5 minutes to dissolve the sugar.

4 Transfer the mixture to an 18- by 13-inch rimmed baking pan and spread the peaches in an even layer. The pan will be full, so be careful when moving it.

5 Bake for 1½ hours, stirring every 30 minutes with a silicone spatula, making sure the peaches around the edges and in the corners get mixed to the center, as they will start to caramelize first. After each stirring, spread the peaches back into an even layer that fills the entire pan.

6 Bake for 10 to 30 minutes longer, stirring every 10 minutes during this final leg of cooking. The jam is done when it is thick and has a glassy appearance; it will thicken more once cool.

7 **To freeze:** Cool before freezing. Because jam is thick, it will pack best in rigid containers.

NOTE: *You can also make this jam with frozen peaches that have been thawed.*

Sweet Bourbon Baked Peaches

While I'll never turn down a good pie, cobbler, or fruit crisp, I also appreciate a dessert that is simple and a bit lighter. Tender, sweet peaches swimming in a bourbon-brown sugar sauce are just that. Try them over yogurt, vanilla ice cream, or angel food cake . . . or simply in a bowl with a drizzle of heavy cream.

YIELD: 6 SERVINGS

- 6 cups frozen peeled and sliced peaches
- 2 tablespoons bourbon
- 2 tablespoons firmly packed brown sugar or maple syrup
- 2 tablespoons finely chopped pecans (optional)

1 Preheat the oven to 375°F (190°C).

2 Place the frozen peaches in an 8- or 9-inch square baking pan and evenly distribute the bourbon and sugar over the top. Sprinkle on the pecans, if using.

3 Cover the pan tightly with aluminum foil and bake for 30 minutes.

4 Remove the foil and bake the peaches for 1 hour longer, or until they are tender and bubbling.

TIP: *Don't like bourbon? Leave it out and add a dash of cinnamon instead!*

Peach BBQ Sauce

This very thick sauce, with a peach-forward flavor and just a touch of heat, goes well on anything grilled or smoked!

YIELD: ABOUT 2 CUPS

- 2 teaspoons extra-virgin olive oil, avocado oil, or lard
- 1 medium yellow onion, diced
- 1 jalapeño, cored, deseeded, and diced
- 4 cups chopped peaches (about 2 pounds whole)
- ½ cup water
- ½ cup sugar
- ¼ cup tomato paste
- ¼ cup apple cider vinegar
- 1 tablespoon molasses
- 1 tablespoon Dijon mustard
- 1 teaspoon sea salt
- 1 teaspoon chili powder
- ½ teaspoon freshly ground black pepper
- ½ teaspoon granulated garlic
- ½ teaspoon ground ginger
- ½ teaspoon smoked paprika
- ⅛ teaspoon cayenne pepper

1 Heat the oil in a medium saucepan over medium heat. Add the onion and jalapeño, and sauté until they are tender, about 7 minutes.

2 Stir in the peaches, water, sugar, tomato paste, vinegar, molasses, mustard, salt, chili powder, black pepper, garlic, ginger, paprika, and cayenne.

3 Gently simmer until the peaches are soft and the mixture has thickened, about 20 minutes.

4 Cool to a safe handling temperature, then use an immersion blender or transfer to a countertop blender and blend on high until very smooth.

5 **To freeze:** Chill the sauce overnight in the refrigerator before freezing, so that the flavors can meld. Because it is thick, barbecue sauce packs best in rigid containers.

PEARS

A perfectly ripe pear can have flavor notes that range from citrus and melon to vanilla and cinnamon. Most pears need a period of time to ripen off the tree, so if your pears are too firm or underwhelming in flavor, give them a few days on the counter to develop. You can check a pear's ripeness by gently pressing your thumb into the neck near the stem. If it gives a little, the pear is ready.

Freezing Raw Pears

Raw pears will become very soft and fall-apart-mushy once thawed, so they aren't well suited for baking—but they excel at making pear sauce or pear butter. For firm pears that hold their shape after being frozen, bake them first, following the directions on the opposite page for Versatile Plain Baked Pears.

Prep. Peel or not—it's up to you. If the pears are intended for blending, I leave the peels on; otherwise I peel them before freezing.

Remove the stems, cut the pears in half, then use a melon baller or small spoon to remove the core in the center. Pears can be frozen in halves, quarters, slices, or smaller pieces.

Freeze. Pears pack best in freezer bags. Consider flash freezing pears to use in smaller quantities. Because pears will brown when exposed to air, work in batches and get them into the freezer as soon as they are ready.

Special thawing instructions. As the pears are thawing, they will release a lot of liquid. Make sure to save this juice, as it's packed with flavor. The easiest way to collect the juice is to hold the freezer bag over a bowl, snip off a corner, and let the liquid drain into the bowl.

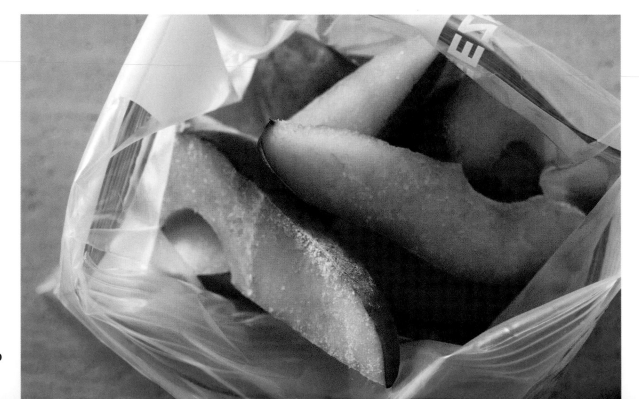

Cinnamon Baked Pears

Pears fare better when cooked before being frozen, so filling them with cinnamon and sugar before baking is a clever and handy way to preserve them. The thawed pears hold their shape remarkably well. They can be served warm or cold—try them sprinkled with toasted nuts and served with a scoop of yogurt for breakfast.

YIELD: 6 SERVINGS

  6 large pears, any variety

  1 tablespoon firmly packed brown sugar or maple sugar

  1 teaspoon ground cinnamon

    Pinch of sea salt

  ¼ cup water

1 Preheat the oven to 375°F (190°C).

2 Cut the pears in half from top to bottom, then use a melon baller or small spoon to scoop out the seed cavity. Cut a thin slice off the rounded backside of each pear half so that the fruit sits level, and arrange the halves in a 13- by 9-inch baking pan.

3 Stir together the sugar, cinnamon, and salt in a small bowl, then divide the mixture evenly among the pears, sprinkling it all over the exposed cut side.

4 Pour the water into the bottom of the pan, and cover the pan tightly with aluminum foil. Bake for 45 to 50 minutes, or until the pears are soft.

5 **To freeze:** Cool before freezing. Flash freeze the pear halves, then transfer to a freezer bag for storage.

Variation: Versatile Plain Baked Pears

Pears that are baked before freezing will be firm and hold their shape very well once thawed. This makes them useful for dicing into pieces and adding to muffins and other baked goods. Follow the instructions for Cinnamon Baked Pears, but omit the brown sugar, cinnamon, and salt in step 3.

Vanilla Pear Sauce

Both floral and complex, pears and vanilla are an amazing duo. Using a vanilla bean will add those fancy little black flecks, but vanilla extract will taste just as lovely. I prefer a chunky pear sauce, so I peel the pears before cooking. If you'd like to include the skins, follow the general directions for Smooth Applesauce on page 42—that technique works with pears too.

YIELD: ABOUT 7 CUPS

16 cups peeled and chopped pears (about 12 large whole)

½ vanilla bean or 2 teaspoons vanilla extract

Pinch of sea salt

1 Pour ⅛ inch of water into a large pot, then add the pears. Cover and cook over medium-low heat for 10 minutes.

2 Split the vanilla bean in half lengthwise, and use the tip of a small knife to scrape out all the seeds. (If using vanilla extract, add it in step 4 instead.)

3 Stir the salt, vanilla bean seeds, and the empty pod into the pear mixture. Cook, uncovered, stirring occasionally, until the pears are soft and easily mashed and their liquid is reduced, about 30 minutes.

4 Remove the vanilla pod, then use a handheld masher to mash the pears into a chunky sauce. If using vanilla extract, add it now.

5 **To freeze:** Cool before freezing. Pear sauce packs well in freezer bags or rigid containers.

Salty Caramel Pear Butter

Imagine a pear butter so thick and sweet that you just may mistake it for a salted caramel sauce! Spread it on toast, bagels, and English muffins, or spoon it over ice cream.

YIELD: ABOUT 3½ CUPS

- 16 cups chopped pears, in 1- to 2-inch chunks (about 12 large whole; see Note)
- 1 cup water
- ½ cup firmly packed brown sugar
- 2 teaspoons vanilla extract
- ½ teaspoon sea salt

1 Combine the pears, water, sugar, vanilla, and salt in a 6-quart slow cooker. Cover and cook on high for 2 hours.

2 Give the pears a good stir, then cook until they are soft and easily mashed, about 2 hours longer.

3 Allow the pears to cool to a safe handling temperature, then use an immersion blender or transfer to a countertop blender and blend on high until smooth. Work in batches, if needed.

4 Return the puréed pears to the slow cooker and cook on high, uncovered, for 4 to 5 hours, stirring every hour, until the pear butter is so thick that a large spoonful sticks to the spoon when held upside down. It's okay if the pear butter forms a skin on top between stirrings—just mix it in.

5 **To freeze:** Cool before freezing. Because it is thick, pear butter packs best in rigid containers. A little goes a long way with pear butter, so I prefer to freeze this in small containers.

NOTE: *There's no need to peel the pears for this recipe. If using frozen pears, thaw the pears first and include all the liquid they release. Reduce the water in step 1 to ¼ cup.*

Variation: Simple Unsweetened Pear Butter

A simple pear butter with no added sugar is also naturally sweet, flavorful, and just as easy to make. Follow the instructions for Salty Caramel Pear Butter, but omit the brown sugar and vanilla, and reduce the sea salt to ⅛ teaspoon.

PEAS

There isn't a more whimsical vegetable than peas, if you ask me. With their curlicue tendrils, colorful flowers, and drooping pods, peas always make the garden feel like an enchanted place.

Freezing Shelling Peas

First things first: Get your peas and find a comfy spot, preferably an old rocking chair on a covered porch. The act of shelling peas is one of those old-fashioned activities that takes a bit of time but is good for the soul.

Prep. To shell peas, snap off the very tip of the pod, which will reveal the fibrous string holding the two sides of the pod together. Pull this string downward, unzipping the pod. Some pods are stringless, and if that's the case, simply pop them open. Slide your thumb along the inside of the pod to dislodge the peas, allowing them to fall into your collection bowl.

Blanch. Blanch peas for 2 minutes in boiling water (preferred; see page 12). Alternatively, steam blanch (see page 10) for 3 minutes, tossing the peas around after 90 seconds. Move them immediately to an ice bath and chill for 2 minutes. Drain as much water from the peas as possible, then transfer to a towel-lined pan to dry.

Freeze. Peas pack best in freezer bags. There is no need to flash freeze peas, as they can be easily separated when frozen together.

Freezing Snow Peas & Snap Peas

Pea pods make for an easy side dish simply topped with butter and salt, and they're a staple veggie in stir-fries. Pea pods will be limp but crunchy once thawed, so use them in cooked dishes.

Prep. If the pea pods have tough strings, or stem caps still attached, remove them before blanching.

Blanch. Steam blanch (preferred; see page 10) for 3 minutes, tossing the pea pods around at the 90-second mark. Alternatively, blanch for 2 minutes in boiling water (see page 12). Move immediately to an ice bath and chill for 2 minutes. Drain as much water from the pea pods as possible, then transfer to a towel-lined pan to dry.

Freeze. Pea pods pack best in freezer bags.

TYPES OF PEAS

There are three main types of peas: shelling, snap, and snow, and each has its own personality. Shelling peas are grown for the sweet peas inside and have a tough outer pod that is removed and discarded. Snap peas have an edible pod with big, sweet peas inside and are usually eaten fresh, but can also be frozen. Snow peas are most commonly used for cooking, but are good for fresh eating too. They are flatter with less prominent peas inside the pod and are a great candidate for freezing.

Creamy Sweet Pea Hummus

A combination of chickpeas and sweet green peas makes for a brightly flavored, creamy hummus. Serve with fresh veggies, crackers, pretzels, or toasted pita wedges.

YIELD: 2 CUPS

- 1 (15-ounce) can chickpeas
- 1 cup frozen green peas, thawed
- 1 small garlic clove, minced
- 2 tablespoons finely grated Parmesan cheese (optional)
- 1 tablespoon extra-virgin olive oil
- 1 tablespoon fresh lemon juice
- ½ teaspoon sea salt

1 Drain the chickpeas and reserve the liquid.

2 Place the chickpeas, green peas, garlic, Parmesan (if using), oil, lemon juice, and salt in a food processor. Process until all the ingredients are chopped up finely, stopping to scrape down the sides of the bowl as necessary.

3 Add 1 tablespoon of the reserved chickpea liquid at a time, processing between each addition, until you reach your desired consistency. (I generally use 2 to 3 tablespoons.) The hummus should flow freely. Store in the refrigerator in an airtight container.

Shrimp & Pea Pod Stir-Fry

This is one of my "I didn't plan for dinner" dinners. Shrimp and snow or snap peas are quick to thaw, and I always have them stashed in the freezer. A simple combination of seafood and veggies in a light, garlicky soy glaze, this dish comes together with little effort and always hits the spot.

YIELD: 3–4 SERVINGS

- 1 tablespoon extra-virgin olive oil, avocado oil, or lard
- 1 large carrot, sliced into thin coins
- 1 pound raw shrimp, peeled, deveined, and tails removed
- 2 cups frozen snow or snap peas, thawed
- 1 garlic clove, minced
- ¼ cup soy sauce
- 3 tablespoons cold water
- 1 tablespoon cornstarch
- ¼ teaspoon crushed red pepper
- ⅛ teaspoon ground ginger
- Cooked white or brown rice, for serving (optional)

1 Heat the oil in a large skillet over medium-high heat. Add the carrot and sauté until almost tender, about 5 minutes.

2 Add the shrimp, pea pods, and garlic, and cook, stirring frequently, until the shrimp are nearly cooked through, about 5 minutes.

3 Whisk together the soy sauce, water, cornstarch, crushed red pepper, and ginger in a small bowl. Stream this mixture slowly into the shrimp and veggies while stirring.

4 Cook, stirring continuously, until the sauce has thickened, about 2 minutes. Serve over rice, if desired.

Potluck Ranch Pasta Salad

This dish is a throwback to the cuisine of my childhood with noodles, peas, ham, and cheddar held together with a ranch-seasoned mayo dressing. It's not a proper picnic or potluck without a creamy pasta salad! This recipe doubles easily if you're feeding a bigger crowd.

YIELD: 6-8 SERVINGS

- 8 ounces dry medium pasta shells
- ½ cup mayonnaise
- ¼ cup whole or 2% milk
- ½ teaspoon sugar
- 2 teaspoons dried parsley
- ½ teaspoon granulated onion
- ½ teaspoon granulated garlic
- ½ teaspoon dried dill
- ½ teaspoon sea salt
- ½ cup frozen green peas, thawed
- ½ cup diced cooked ham
- ½ cup diced mild cheddar cheese

1 Boil the pasta according to the package directions, but don't use any salt in the cooking water. Drain the pasta and rinse it under cold water, then allow it to drain well.

2 Whisk together the mayonnaise, milk, sugar, parsley, onion, garlic, dill, and salt in a large bowl. Fold in the peas, ham, cheese, and pasta and mix until well combined.

3 Refrigerate the pasta salad for 15 minutes before serving.

NOTE: *If the salad sits longer than about 30 minutes, the noodles will start to absorb the dressing and will appear dry. So, if you need to make this dish ahead of time, pour the dressing in the bottom of a serving bowl, then layer on the peas, ham, cheese, and finally the cooked pasta. Cover tightly and refrigerate for up to 1 day. Stir and fold everything together 15 minutes before serving.*

PEPPERS

Because of their endless variety of colors, shapes, and flavors, peppers have become one of my favorite crops to grow. I always grow a unique assortment, from purple bell peppers to those with tie-dye-looking stripes, and even ones shaped like flying saucers! Picking a basketful of bright, shiny peppers always feels special.

Freezing Sweet & Hot Pepper Slices

Whether frozen raw or blanched, peppers will be limp when thawed, so they work best in dishes that are cooked. Raw peppers will develop a slightly different flavor when frozen (not bad, but different). Raw peppers are quicker to preserve, but they won't keep as long in the freezer. Blanched peppers will have a more muted pepper flavor than raw but will keep longer; I prefer to blanch.

Prep. For larger peppers such as sweet bells, remove the stem, seeds, and ribs, then cut the peppers into strips about ½ inch thick. I prefer strips because they have less surface area, which means less opportunity for freezer burn. I can always cut the slices into smaller pieces when I use them.

For smaller peppers, such as most hot varieties, cut them into rings or large pieces about ½ inch thick. If you want to make the peppers milder, remove the seeds and ribs.

Blanch. Steam blanch (see page 10) for 2 minutes, tossing the peppers around at the 1-minute mark. Do not use an ice bath. Drain as much water as possible, then spread the warm peppers on a towel-lined pan to cool and dry.

Freeze. Peppers pack best in freezer bags. Consider flash freezing peppers to use in smaller quantities.

Freezing Fire-Roasted Peppers

Take a plump, fresh pepper and char it with flames—now you've got something! Roasting accomplishes the same goal as blanching, plus it adds flavor. My favorite peppers for roasting are poblanos and sweet red bell peppers, although any large sweet pepper will work. Add roasted peppers to pasta, hummus, slow-cooker meals, eggs, soups, and more.

Prep. Cut off the tops of the peppers, cut the peppers in half from top to bottom, then remove the ribs and seeds. Peppers can be roasted on a grill or under the broiler in an oven. The goal is to char the peppers quickly but not overcook them.

For grilling, preheat the grill to high and place the pepper halves skin-side down directly on the grill grates. Grill with the lid open until the peppers are charred on the skin side, 5 to 7 minutes. Remove any peppers that finish blackening before the others.

For oven broiling, preheat the broiler and place the pepper halves skin-side up on a baking pan (do not use parchment paper). Place the pan about 6 inches away from the broiler and cook for 5 to 7 minutes, or until the peppers have fully charred on the top. Rotate the pan so that the peppers char evenly, and remove any peppers that finish blackening before the others.

No matter which method you choose, after being charred, the skin will start to peel off. When the peppers have cooled to a safe handling temperature, peel away the blackened skin—it's okay if you can't get it all. You'll now be left with tender, smoky roasted peppers.

Freeze. Cool before freezing. Fire-roasted peppers pack best in freezer bags. Consider flash freezing peppers to use in smaller quantities. Fire-roasted peppers can also be puréed in a food processor and frozen.

❄ FOR THE FREEZER
Chili Starter

Peppers were one of the first foods I ever preserved the year I started growing heirloom veggies in my own garden. I had so many peppers, I didn't know what to do with them! Chili starter was the perfect solution, and it makes quick work of putting on a pot of chili (see the recipe on page 142). The following combination is my tried-and-true favorite, but the recipe is versatile, so feel free to use whatever you like (or grow) for your chili. This recipe easily scales up to make multiple batches of starter.

YIELD: ENOUGH FOR 1 BATCH OF CHILI

- 1 cup diced green bell pepper
- ¾ cup diced yellow or red bell pepper, or poblano
- ¼ cup cored, deseeded, and finely diced jalapeño

1 Toss all the peppers together, or simply layer them into freezer containers.

2 **To freeze:** Chili starter packs well in freezer bags or rigid containers.

Variation: Chili Starter with Onions & Celery

If you have onions and celery that need preserving, add about 1 cup of each to this mix before freezing. Just be sure to label the bag so you know what's in it when it comes time to make chili. If using this starter in the Midwestern Chili on page 142, omit step 2 and simply add the chili starter in step 3.

Candied Jalapeño Slices

For years I've made hot pepper jelly with jalapeños—you know that stuff you pour over a log of cream cheese and serve with crackers for the fanciest appetizer you ever did see? Well, I started making candied jalapeño slices instead, and I won't go back to the jelly! These addictively sweet-and-spicy peppers can be used in the exact same way, but they're more versatile—try them on burgers, scrambled eggs, or tacos.

YIELD: ABOUT 3 CUPS

- 1 cup sugar
- ½ cup distilled white vinegar
- ¼ cup apple cider vinegar
- ½ teaspoon sea salt
- ½ teaspoon granulated garlic
- ½ teaspoon dried oregano
- 8 cups sliced jalapeños, in ⅛-inch-thick rounds (about 1½ pounds whole; see Note)

1 Combine the sugar, vinegars, salt, garlic, and oregano in a medium pot. Bring to a simmer over medium heat, then add the jalapeños. Simmer, stirring frequently, until the jalapeños are limp and become submerged in the liquid, about 5 minutes.

2 Continue cooking, stirring occasionally, until the jalapeños appear shriveled and the liquid in the bottom of the pan is almost gone, 15 to 20 minutes longer.

3 **To freeze:** Cool before freezing. Spoon the jalapeños and their syrup into freezer containers. Because they are sticky, candied jalapeños pack best in rigid containers.

NOTE: *For a milder version (these are spicy!), use a pepper corer, or cut the peppers in half lengthwise and use a spoon to scrape out the seeds and ribs before cutting into slices.*

Bacon-Wrapped Jalapeño Poppers

If you've found yourself with a glut of jalapeños (as we gardeners inevitably do), these poppers are a homestead favorite! Here's a tip: Taste test your jalapeños first. Sometimes I have a plant that produces wildly hot jalapeños, and I avoid using those in this recipe. Mild ones work best here—unless you like a lot of heat. Hot peppers tend to get hotter the longer they stay on the plant, so for this recipe, harvest as soon as they've reached a good size. Use the largest peppers you have. You'll also need a handful of round toothpicks for this recipe.

YIELD: 28–32 POPPERS

14-16	medium-large jalapeños
1	(8-ounce) package cream cheese, softened
1	tablespoon grated Parmesan cheese
1	teaspoon dried oregano
1	teaspoon granulated garlic
1	teaspoon granulated onion
½	teaspoon sea salt
1	cup shredded sharp cheddar cheese
12-16	ounces thinly sliced bacon

1 Cut the jalapeños in half from top to bottom, cutting close to the stem so that the stem remains intact with one side of the jalapeño. Use a spoon to scrape out the seeds and ribs, working gently so you don't puncture or break the walls of the jalapeños.

2 Mix together the cream cheese, Parmesan, oregano, garlic, onion, and salt in a bowl. Once combined, stir in the cheddar.

3 Fill each jalapeño half with enough of the cream cheese mixture so that it's flush with the top of the pepper but not overflowing.

4 Assemble a test popper before cutting all the bacon to size. Most bacon strips can be cut into thirds, but if your bacon is shorter, you may need to cut it in half. The goal is to wrap the bacon so that it passes under the bottom of the jalapeño once and over the top twice.

5 Cut the bacon into slices about 4 inches long. Wrap a bacon piece around a jalapeño half, stretching the meat gently as you go and making sure the bacon doesn't overlap. Use two toothpicks per popper, one to secure each end of the bacon. Each toothpick should pierce only one wall of the jalapeño; trying to pierce both walls with the same toothpick squishes the popper too much.

6 Place the assembled popper on a parchment paper-lined pan. Repeat until you've worked through all of the jalapeños and bacon. If you run out of bacon before jalapeños, go ahead and leave some without— the poppers cook up fine without the bacon!

7 **To freeze:** Flash freeze the poppers, then transfer to a freezer bag for storage. Take care that the toothpicks don't poke holes in the bag.

8 **To heat:** Preheat the oven to 400°F (200°C).

9 Place the frozen jalapeño poppers in a single layer on a parchment paper-lined pan. Make sure they are cheese-side up and as level as possible. Bake for 30 minutes, or until the bacon is brown and crispy.

NOTE: *Always wear gloves when working with this many hot peppers, and consider protective eyewear as well.*

Midwestern Chili

They say you can tell where a person is from by the type of chili they like. If that's true, it's fairly obvious that I'm from the Midwest. My favorite chili has diced tomatoes, ground beef, and kidney beans in a richly spiced tomato broth, with a helping of cheese and sour cream on top. And it's served with buttered soda crackers, of course! Make this chili with frozen Chili Starter, or use the same amount of fresh peppers.

YIELD: 6–8 SERVINGS

- 2 tablespoons extra-virgin olive oil, avocado oil, or lard
- 2 pounds lean ground beef
- 1 medium yellow onion, diced
- 3 celery stalks, diced
- 4 cups water
- 1 (14.5-ounce) can diced tomatoes
- 1 (14.5-ounce) can crushed tomatoes
- 1 bag frozen Chili Starter (page 139), thawed
- 3 garlic cloves, minced
- ⅓ cup mild chili powder
- 2 teaspoons dried oregano
- 1 teaspoon sea salt
- 1 (16-ounce) can kidney beans, drained and rinsed

1 Heat 1 tablespoon of the oil in a skillet over medium heat. Add the beef and cook, stirring and chopping it into small pieces, until browned, about 10 minutes. Drain any excess fat, and set the meat aside.

2 Heat the remaining 1 tablespoon olive oil in a large pot over medium heat. Add the onion and celery, and sauté until tender, about 7 minutes.

3 Stir in the water, diced tomatoes, crushed tomatoes, chili starter, garlic, chili powder, oregano, and salt. Simmer, uncovered, for 1 hour.

4 Stir in the beans and cook for 5 minutes longer.

TIP: *Chili always tastes better on the second day, after an overnight stay in the refrigerator, so make this dish ahead of time if you're really trying to impress!*

PINEAPPLE

A ripe, juicy pineapple is almost intoxicating, and thankfully it can be frozen with great results. Partially thawed frozen pineapple is an icy treat on a hot summer's day, and it can be used in blended drinks.

Freezing Pineapple Pieces

Prep. Use a sharp knife to cut the top and bottom off the pineapple. With the pineapple standing upright, slice off the brown outer peel, making sure to cut deeply enough to remove the eyes and reveal the yellow flesh beneath. In the center is the core; cut the pineapple away from the core in several large slabs. Dice the slabs into 1-inch pieces.

Freeze. Flash freeze pineapple pieces, then transfer to a freezer bag for storage. Pineapple pieces can also be packed together into freezer containers for use in larger quantities.

Pineapple Whip Ice Pops

Combining pineapple and ice cream in the blender transforms them into a treat that is equally fun and refreshing. Using already-frozen pineapple instead of fresh helps give these ice pops an extra creamy texture.

YIELD: 6–8 ICE POPS

  2 cups frozen pineapple pieces

¾ cup pineapple juice

  1 cup vanilla ice cream

1 Combine the pineapple, pineapple juice, and ice cream in a blender. Blend on high until smooth, about 30 seconds. The mixture will be thick, and you may need to stop periodically to scrape down the sides of the blender and to push down the ingredients.

2 Pour into ice pop molds and freeze until firm.

PLUMS

Biting into a juicy, ripe plum is one of life's finest pleasures. If you don't smell the fruit's fragrant floral notes and juice doesn't run down your chin when you sink your teeth into it, your plums likely need to ripen a bit more.

Freezing Plum Halves

Frozen plums are superb for baking, turning into sauce, or eating partially thawed as a snack. As with other stone fruits, plums will either be clingstone or freestone, which tells you whether the seed in the middle will stick tightly to the flesh or pop out easily.

Prep. For freestone plums, cut them in half from top to bottom and remove the pit. For clingstone plums, cut the flesh away from the pit in several large pieces. I prefer to freeze plums in halves because halves are the most versatile and can always be cut smaller once thawed.

Freeze. Flash freeze plum halves, then transfer to a freezer bag for storage. Plum halves or pieces can also be packed into freezer containers for use in larger quantities.

Buttery Cinnamon Plum Sauce

Every summer when I was growing up, my mom would make a special meal of "plum dumplings" following a recipe passed down from my great-grandmother. The dumplings were prepared by wrapping whole prune plums with dough and boiling them until soft. They were then served topped with a warm and buttery cinnamon plum sauce, which was the real star! This sauce is satisfying eaten by itself, swirled into oatmeal or yogurt, or served over vanilla ice cream along with a sprinkle of granola or crumbled shortbread cookies.

YIELD: ABOUT 6 CUPS

- 2 tablespoons water
- 9 cups chopped plums (about 3 pounds whole)
- ½ cup sugar or honey
- 2 tablespoons butter
- 1 teaspoon ground cinnamon
- Pinch of sea salt

1 Pour the water in a medium pot, then add the plums. Cover and cook over medium heat, stirring occasionally, until the plums are soft and juicy, about 20 minutes.

2 Stir in the sugar, butter, cinnamon, and salt. Simmer until the plums are thick and saucy, about 12 minutes.

3 **To freeze:** Cool before freezing. Plum sauce packs well in freezer bags or rigid containers.

Asian-Inspired Plum Dipping Sauce

I find most store-bought plum sauces to be heavy on the sugar and lacking in plum flavor. Not this one! Homemade plum sauce doesn't skimp on the plums and is sweet and spicy with a hint of vinegar . . . everything you want for dipping fried foods such as egg rolls and wontons or for serving with roasted and grilled meats.

YIELD: ABOUT 4 CUPS

    6 cups chopped plums (about 2 pounds whole)
    ½ medium yellow onion, chopped
    4 garlic cloves, minced
    ½ cup apple cider vinegar
    ½ cup firmly packed brown sugar
    2 tablespoons granulated sugar
    2 tablespoons soy sauce
    1 tablespoon grated fresh ginger
    1 teaspoon sea salt
    ¼ teaspoon crushed red pepper

1 Combine the plums, onion, garlic, vinegar, sugars, soy sauce, ginger, salt, and crushed red pepper in a medium saucepan. Cover and cook over medium heat, stirring occasionally, until the plums are tender and the mixture has thickened, about 20 minutes.

2 Cool to a safe handling temperature, then use an immersion blender or transfer to a countertop blender and blend on high until smooth.

3 **To freeze:** Chill the plum sauce overnight in the refrigerator before freezing, so that the flavors can meld. Because it is thick, plum sauce packs best in rigid containers.

Plum Fruit Leather

Plums make a tasty and stunning fruit leather—one of my favorites, in fact! I prefer to use a dehydrator to dry the fruit purée, but an oven set low will work too. And making fruit leather is a fantastic use of frozen fruit! After making fruit leathers of all types for many years, I've nailed down some universal truths when it comes to mastering this fruity treat: Cooking the fruit and adding some apple to the mix gives it a pleasant texture that prevents it from being actually as tough as leather. Using a bit of honey adds sweetness and makes the fruit leather more pliable.

YIELD: 20 SERVINGS

    6 cups frozen chopped plums, thawed
    2 cups chopped apples, fresh or thawed frozen
    ¼ cup water
    ⅛ teaspoon sea salt
    ⅓ cup honey, plus more as needed

1 Combine the plums, apples, water, and salt in a medium pot. Cover and cook over medium heat, stirring occasionally, until the fruit starts to soften and release its juices, about 15 minutes.

2 Continue cooking, uncovered, stirring ocassionally, until the plums are soft, about 10 minutes. Remove from the heat and stir in the honey.

3 Allow the fruit to cool to a safe handling temperature, then use an immersion blender or transfer to a countertop blender and blend on high until smooth. Taste the purée. It should taste sweet and pleasant. If it doesn't, blend in small amounts of honey until it's to your liking.

Recipe continues on next page

4

4 If using a dehydrator, pour the fruit purée onto dehydrator trays lined with fruit leather sheets; for oven-drying, pour the purée onto large baking pans lined with parchment paper. Use the back of a spoon to spread the purée into a thin, even layer. If your dehydrator has a temperature control, set it to 130°F (55°C); if using the oven, set it to 150°F (65°C). Many variables can affect drying time, so dehydrate until the purée is no longer tacky to the touch. If using the oven, be careful not to overcook the purée or you may end up with fruit brittle instead of leather.

5 When dry, cut into strips, roll them up, and store in an airtight container.

POTATOES

Potatoes are one of my favorite crops to grow, and digging the spuds out of the ground every fall feels like digging for gold! One glance at the frozen foods section of any grocery store tells you that potatoes freeze wonderfully in many different preparations and are a treasured freezer staple. Potatoes should be at least parcooked or blanched before freezing; otherwise they can discolor and become grainy or disintegrate once thawed.

Freezing Shredded Potatoes

Use waxy or all-purpose potatoes, and, if possible, choose ones that are similar in size so that they cook evenly. Leave the potatoes whole, and do not peel them. The skins help hold the potatoes together while shredding, and they mostly fall off during the shredding process anyway.

Prep. Place cleaned, whole potatoes in a large pot and fill it with cold water to 2 inches above the potatoes. Bring to a boil over medium heat, and simmer until the potatoes are tender, 20 to 30 minutes depending on their size. To test doneness, stick a fork into the middle of a potato. If it is easy to pierce, it's done. Do not overcook; slightly underdone is better than overdone.

Drain the potatoes and chill them in the refrigerator for at least 4 hours, although overnight is best. The potatoes must be completely cool, otherwise they won't shred nicely.

Use a box grater to shred potatoes, and take care to gently but firmly press them into the grater. This will ensure you get nice, big shreds and not small crumbles. I don't like to use a food processor for this task, as it produces smaller, more crumbly shreds.

Freeze. Shredded potatoes pack well in freezer bags or rigid containers.

Heat. For crispy hash browns, use a generous amount of fat; I prefer butter, olive oil, or lard. Heat a large skillet over medium heat and add enough fat to just coat the bottom of the pan. Add thawed shredded potatoes in a layer up to ½ inch thick. Allow the hash browns to cook on the first side until golden and crispy, about 8 minutes. Flip and cook on the second side until crispy, 5 to 7 minutes. Sprinkle generously with salt.

Freezing French Fries

As a French fry connoisseur, I want my fries to be golden brown and crispy on the outside and pillowy on the inside . . . even better if they can be baked in the oven. Seems like a tall order, but these fries hit all those marks!

Unlike store-bought frozen fries that are flash frozen individually, home-frozen fries are easiest to pack together in a freezer bag and then thaw before baking. This thawing step is probably different than what you're used to when cooking store-bought frozen fries. These fries will feel limp once thawed, but they will turn out like something you'd get at a high-end steak house!

Russet potatoes are the best choice for fries, although all-purpose varieties will work too. Waxy potatoes are not recommended.

Prep. Scrub and peel the potatoes, then cut them lengthwise into sticks about ½ inch thick. This will seem large, but it's what works best for oven-baked fries that are pillowy inside and crisp on the outside.

Blanch. Blanch fries for 3 minutes in boiling water (see page 12). Move immediately to an ice bath and chill for 3 minutes. Drain as much water from the fries as possible, then transfer to a towel-lined pan to dry.

Freeze. Fries pack best in freezer bags. You can flash freeze fries, but I find it to be unnecessary and impractical, especially when processing a large quantity.

Heat. The fries should be thawed before baking; it's okay if they're still a little icy, as long as they can be separated. Preheat the oven to 425°F (220°C) and rub a thin layer of extra-virgin olive oil on a large baking pan. Use a towel to pat the fries dry, then spread them on the pan in a single layer. Drizzle more olive oil over the fries (about 2 tablespoons for a quart bag of fries) and gently toss them to coat. Sprinkle generously with salt, then bake for about 45 minutes, or until golden brown.

All-purpose potatoes

Waxy potatoes

Starchy potatoes

TYPES OF POTATOES

There are three main types of potatoes, and being familiar with them and their optimal uses will ensure success in the kitchen. This is especially important when freezing them.

Starchy potatoes are low in moisture and high in starch. This type of potato makes excellent fries. They tend to break down easily, which makes them a great choice for puréed soups. Starchy potatoes are good at absorbing cream and butter, which means they make the best mashed potatoes. The most familiar starchy potato is the russet.

Waxy potatoes are lower in starch and have a firm texture. Their sturdy flesh makes them the best choice for boiling in water for dishes such as potato salad or diced for use in soups. Because they hold their shape well, waxy potatoes make crispy hash browns. New potatoes, most red-skinned potatoes, and fingerlings fall under the category of waxy potatoes.

All-purpose potatoes are somewhere in the middle and do well for most preparations. This is my favorite type of potato for roasting and using in soups and stews. The most well-known potato variety in this category is Yukon Gold.

Garlic Mashed Potatoes

I prefer my mashed potatoes rustic and lumpy with plenty of butter and garlic! Frozen mashed potatoes have a reputation for sometimes being grainy. Although the texture won't be exactly like fresh, these reheat well and turn out smooth when following the reheating technique outlined below. Mashed potatoes can also be frozen plain without the butter and half-and-half. To do so, simply follow the same general instructions and add those ingredients upon reheating if you like.

YIELD: 12 SERVINGS

- 3 pounds starchy or all-purpose potatoes
- 4 tablespoons butter
- 2 garlic cloves, minced
- 1 teaspoon sea salt
- ¾ cup half-and-half or whole milk

1 Scrub and peel the potatoes, then cut them into approximately 2-inch pieces. Place them in a large pot and fill it with cold water to about 2 inches above the potatoes.

2 Bring to a boil over medium heat and simmer until the potatoes are tender, about 20 minutes. When the potatoes are easy to pierce with a fork, they're done.

3 Meanwhile, melt the butter in a small saucepan over low heat. Add the garlic and sauté until fragrant but not browning, about 4 minutes. Remove from the heat and allow the garlic to continue steeping in the butter.

4 Drain the potatoes and immediately return them to the pot. Add the garlic butter and salt, and use a handheld masher to mash the potatoes until they are almost smooth.

5 Use a whisk to incorporate the half-and-half while giving the potatoes a light final whipping.

6 **To freeze:** Cool before freezing. Mashed potatoes pack well in freezer bags or rigid containers. Consider freezing individual portions in a silicone muffin pan.

7 **To heat:** Thaw potatoes, then place them in a saucepan over medium-low heat and cook, stirring occasionally, until they are warmed through, 5 to 10 minutes depending on quantity. Use a silicone spatula to fold the potatoes around the pan, forcing them against the sides, which will reduce graininess. Thawed potatoes can also be heated in the microwave or in a covered casserole dish in the oven. Or try them on shepherd's pie!

Loaded Twice-Baked Potatoes

You will thank yourself for taking the time to put these up! Even if you don't have potatoes that need to be preserved, twice-baked potatoes are a valuable make-ahead item for whipping up a quick dinner. The texture of these potatoes is smooth and creamy—not grainy at all. Feel free to add a handful of cooked, crumbled bacon to the filling if you'd like.

YIELD: 12 SERVINGS

- 12 medium russet potatoes (about 5 pounds)
- 2 tablespoons extra-virgin olive oil
- 6 ounces medium cheddar cheese, shredded, plus more for topping (optional)
- ½ cup sour cream
- 4 tablespoons butter, melted
- ⅓ cup chopped fresh chives, plus more for topping (optional)
- 1½ teaspoons sea salt

1 Preheat the oven to 400°F (200°C).

2 Leave the potatoes whole, scrub them clean, and dry them with a towel. Pierce each potato two times with a fork, rub them with a thin layer of the oil, and place them on a baking pan. Bake for 50 to 60 minutes, or until cooked through. Leave the oven on.

3 Allow the potatoes to cool to safe handling temperature, but work while they are still quite warm. (I find it helpful to cradle the potatoes in a clean kitchen towel so I can hold them while they're hot.) Cut each potato in half lengthwise, and use a spoon to scrape out the inside flesh and place it in a large bowl. Leave a ¼-inch layer of flesh intact inside each potato so that the shell doesn't collapse.

4 Once all the potatoes have been hollowed out, mash the potato flesh with a handheld masher. Stir in the cheese, sour cream, butter, chives, and salt.

5 Spoon the mashed potato mixture back into the empty potato shells, dividing it evenly among them. For a prettier potato, top the filling with an extra sprinkle of shredded cheese and chives.

6 Place the filled potatoes back on the pan and bake for 45 minutes, or until the filling is turning golden brown on top.

7 **To freeze:** Cool before freezing. Flash freeze, then transfer to a freezer bag for storage.

8 **To heat:** Thaw twice-baked potatoes, then heat in the microwave for 2 to 3 minutes, or until warm in the center. Alternatively, bake at 350°F (180°C) for 20 minutes, or until warmed through.

FOR THE TABLE

Leftover Mashed Potato Quick Bread

Homemade bread usually requires time and patience, but not this loaf! This bread whips up in a matter of minutes, uses leftover or frozen mashed potatoes, and doesn't require any rising time. Because it is leavened with baking soda, it tastes like a traditional soda bread, but the mashed potatoes give it a terrific buttery flavor. The crust is crunchy and golden, and the interior is dense but soft as a cloud.

YIELD: 10 SERVINGS

4	cups all-purpose flour
1½	teaspoons baking soda
1½	teaspoons sea salt
1½	cups frozen prepared mashed potatoes, thawed
1¼	cups milk
1	egg
2	teaspoons lemon juice
2	tablespoons extra-virgin olive oil

1 Preheat the oven to 425°F (220°C). (Note: It is crucial to bring the oven fully up to temperature before baking. Because the bread is leavened with baking soda, it needs to be shaped and put into a hot oven quickly after the wet and dry ingredients are combined; otherwise it won't rise properly and will become dense.)

2 Whisk together the flour, baking soda, and salt in a large bowl.

3 In another bowl, whisk together the mashed potatoes, milk, egg, and lemon juice.

4 Add the potato mixture into the flour mixture, and stir until well combined. Turn the dough out onto a flat surface and knead until it just comes together, about 1 minute. Don't overknead. The dough will be shaggy.

5 Working quickly, form the dough into a round, slightly domed loaf shape about 6 inches in diameter. It's okay if it has cracks and fissures.

6 Grease the bottom of a cast-iron pan (any size, as long as the loaf doesn't touch the sides) with 1 tablespoon of the oil. Place the loaf in the pan, then rub the top with the remaining 1 tablespoon oil. In the top of the loaf, make two shallow cuts about 4 inches long and in the shape of an X.

7 Bake for 45 to 50 minutes, or until the bread is very golden around the edges. For best results, allow the bread to cool before slicing.

Variation: Herby Mashed Potato Quick Bread

Add 1 tablespoon of fresh herbs to the dry ingredients in step 2. Rosemary, chives, or dill are great options.

RASPBERRIES

My grandmother was an avid gardener, and she had a gorgeous raspberry patch. Her freezer was always full of old Cool Whip and Country Crock containers bursting with homegrown raspberries. I'm sure that's where my love of raspberries comes from. We grow 10 different varieties in all different colors, each one having a slightly different flavor. Raspberries are a freezer staple and one of my favorite summertime treats!

Freezing Whole Raspberries

Prep. Unlike other types of berries, raspberries have a center cavity that bugs like to hide in. I always give the berries a good look over before freezing them so there are no surprises later.

Freeze. Take care to gently pack raspberries into freezer containers; if crushed they will become juicy and stick together. Raspberries pack best in freezer bags. If the raspberries are dry, there is no need to flash freeze them, as they can be separated when frozen together. If your berries are particularly juicy or wet, consider flash freezing.

❄ FOR THE FREEZER

"Almost Seedless" Raspberry Purée

Why "almost seedless"? Call me particular, but I think too many raspberry seeds can easily overwhelm a recipe. On the other hand, I do like a few seeds so that you know it's raspberry . . . thus almost seedless. I use this purée as the base for raspberry jam, fruit leather, and raspberry gelatin. Raspberry purée is tart, so feel free to sweeten it with some sugar or honey and warm it to make a dessert sauce for spooning over ice cream, yogurt, angel food cake, or cheesecake. You can scale this recipe up or down.

YIELD: ¾ CUP

2 cups raspberries, fresh or frozen

1 Pour ⅛ inch of water into a medium pot, then add the raspberries. Bring to a simmer over medium heat, stirring often, until the raspberries become juicy and have broken down, about 12 minutes. As they cook, use a handheld masher to break them apart.

2 Set up a fine-mesh sieve over a large bowl and pour the hot berries into the sieve. Use the back of a soup spoon to stir the berries, scraping them across the bottom of the sieve and working them through the mesh. Keep working the berries until the pulp and juice is in the bowl below and only seeds are left in the sieve. Stop periodically and use a spatula to scrape off and collect any pulp stuck on the bottom of the sieve. Work in batches, if needed. Stir in about ¼ teaspoon seeds.

3 **To freeze:** Raspberry purée packs best in rigid containers. Consider freezing smaller portions in a silicone mold.

Raspberry Coconut Macaroons

These cheery macaroons are soft and moist, a little bit chewy, and full of fresh raspberry flavor. They are a nice, light cookie for warmer months and will add brightness to a holiday cookie platter. The combination of coconut, raspberry, and vanilla is altogether lovely.

YIELD: 15 COOKIES

- 2 cups finely shredded unsweetened coconut
- ½ cup sugar
- 2 tablespoons coconut flour
- ⅛ teaspoon sea salt
- 3 egg whites
- 1 teaspoon vanilla extract
- 1 cup frozen raspberries, thawed

1 Preheat the oven to 325°F (160°C). Line a baking pan with parchment paper.

2 Place the shredded coconut, sugar, coconut flour, and salt in a food processor and process until the coconut is broken down into a finer crumb, 15 to 30 seconds.

3 Add the egg whites and vanilla, and process until well combined, about 15 seconds.

4 Add the raspberries and all of their liquid, and pulse until just combined. Allow the mixture to sit for 10 minutes to hydrate.

5 Use a spring-loaded scoop to portion and pack the mixture into balls of about 1½ tablespoons each, then drop them onto the prepared baking pan. If you don't have a spring-loaded scoop, use your hands to roll the mixture into balls.

6 Bake for 35 to 40 minutes, or until the macaroons are just starting to turn golden brown on the top and bottom. Store cooled macaroons in an airtight container in the refrigerator.

Raspberry Cheesecake Brownies

A little more brownie than cheesecake, and with a generous portion of sweet-tart jammy raspberries swirled in, these are my favorite treats to make when I want to impress someone. They're dense in a wonderful way, and they definitely lean toward the fudgy side of the brownie spectrum.

YIELD: 12 SERVINGS

RASPBERRY SWIRL

1½ cups frozen raspberries

½ cup sugar

1 teaspoon lemon juice

CHEESECAKE BATTER

8 ounces cream cheese, softened

4 tablespoons butter, softened

¼ cup sugar

1 egg

1 tablespoon all-purpose flour or gluten-free flour blend

1 teaspoon vanilla extract

BROWNIE BATTER

¾ cup sugar

2 eggs

¾ cup semisweet chocolate chips, melted

¼ cup water, at room temperature

4 tablespoons butter, melted

1 teaspoon vanilla extract

¾ cup all-purpose flour or gluten-free flour blend

¼ cup unsweetened Dutch-process cocoa powder

½ teaspoon baking powder

½ teaspoon sea salt

1 To make the raspberry swirl, combine the raspberries, sugar, and lemon juice in a small saucepan. Cook over medium heat, stirring continuously, until the raspberries thaw and start to release their juice, about 5 minutes. Continue simmering, stirring occasionally, until the mixture becomes thick and jammy, about 7 minutes longer. Set aside to cool.

2 Preheat the oven to 350°F (180°C). Line the bottom and sides of a 9-inch square metal baking pan with parchment paper.

3 To make the cheesecake batter, place the cream cheese and butter in a large bowl. Using a hand mixer or a stand mixer fitted with a paddle attachment, beat together on medium speed until uniform, about 1 minute. Add the sugar, egg, flour, and vanilla, and beat again until just combined. Set aside.

4 To make the brownie batter, combine the sugar and eggs in a large bowl. Using a hand mixer or stand mixer fitted with a paddle attachment, beat together on medium-high speed until light and creamy, about 3 minutes.

5 Add the melted chocolate, water, butter, and vanilla, and mix again until just combined. Scrape down the sides and bottom of the bowl with a spatula as needed.

6 Whisk together the flour, cocoa powder, baking powder, and salt in a bowl. Add this to the batter and mix on low until just combined; do not overmix.

7 Drop the brownie batter in ¼-cup portions and the cheesecake batter in heaping spoonfuls into the prepared pan, alternating and layering them on top of each other; there's no right or wrong pattern. Next, drop teaspoons of the raspberry jam all around on top of the batter.

8 The batters will be different thicknesses, but that's okay; they can still be swirled together. Use a butter knife to swirl the raspberry and batters around the pan.

9 Bake for 40 to 45 minutes, or until the center is set. Allow the brownies to cool completely before cutting. Store in an airtight container in the refrigerator.

RHUBARB

Nothing says spring like rhubarb because it's often one of the first plants to pop up when the snow melts. Here in the Midwest, it's common for every farm, homestead, and country property to have their own rhubarb patch.

Freezing Rhubarb Pieces

Prep. Cut off and discard the leaves, and cut the rhubarb stalks into 1-inch pieces. There is no need to peel rhubarb, unless it is older and particularly tough or woody. Rhubarb does not require blanching.

Freeze. Rhubarb pieces pack best in freezer bags.

Brown Sugar Roasted Rhubarb

Rhubarb swimming in a brown sugar caramel sauce is my favorite topping for a dish of yogurt. Unlike with a traditional sauced or stewed rhubarb, the pieces hold their shape here—just be careful not to stir them too vigorously after cooking. They have a captivating texture that is dense yet tender, and a lightly sweet and tart taste.

YIELD: 4–5 CUPS

- ½ vanilla bean or 2 teaspoons vanilla extract
- ⅔ cup firmly packed brown sugar or honey
- ¼ teaspoon sea salt
- 8 cups cut rhubarb stalks, in 1-inch pieces (about 2¼ pounds)

1 Preheat the oven to 400°F (200°C).

2 Split the vanilla bean in half lengthwise, and use the tip of a small knife to scrape out all the seeds into a small bowl. Mix together the vanilla bean seeds (or vanilla extract), sugar, and salt.

3 Place the rhubarb in a large bowl. Fold the sugar mixture into the rhubarb, then let it sit 15 minutes to macerate. Stir again, then pour the rhubarb into an 8- or 9-inch square baking pan. Push down the rhubarb pieces, so they are nestled in their juices.

4 Bake for 45 minutes, or until the rhubarb is bubbly and tender.

5 **To freeze:** Cool before freezing. Spoon the rhubarb and its juices into freezer containers. Roasted rhubarb packs best in rigid containers.

STRAWBERRIES

There's nothing better than picking a fresh strawberry still warm from the sun and eating it right there in the garden. Strawberries are such a cheery fruit, and freezing them feels like capturing some of that summer sunshine.

Freezing Whole Strawberries

Prep. Green strawberry tops are edible and have a light grassy flavor, so the berries can be frozen with them on. If you use strawberries only for smoothies, it's less work to keep the caps, and they add extra nutrition. Strawberries meant for cooking and baking should have their green tops removed before freezing.

Freeze. Flash freeze strawberries, then transfer to a freezer bag for storage. Strawberries pack best in freezer bags.

Freezing Sweetened Sliced Strawberries

Macerating fresh strawberries in sugar draws out some of their juice and creates a sweet syrup for them to swim around in. Once thawed they will be soft but not mushy. Use these strawberries on your shortcake or anywhere you need a sweet and fruity dessert topping!

Prep. Remove the green tops, and cut the strawberries into ¼-inch slices. Place the strawberries in a large bowl and stir in 1 tablespoon of sugar for every 1 cup of sliced strawberries. Let the strawberries sit at room temperature for 1 hour, giving them a gentle stir every 15 minutes.

Freeze. Freeze immediately. Sweetened sliced strawberries pack well in bags or rigid containers.

❄ **FOR THE FREEZER**

Strawberry Sun Freezer Jam

Not only is this the best jam I've ever had, it's also one of the easiest (and most fun!) jams I've ever made. Just set your pans in a protected sunny spot (I use the dashboard of my car) and let Mother Nature do most of the work—you don't need to use any pectin. Because this jam isn't cooked on the stove for a long time, it retains a bright, fresh strawberry flavor. Unlike a traditional freezer jam, the flavor is concentrated, which deepens the strawberry taste. It's the best of all worlds! You'll need 5 to 8 hours of full sun on a summer's day to make this jam, so plan accordingly.

YIELD: ABOUT 5 CUPS

- 12 cups fresh or thawed frozen whole strawberries
- 3 cups sugar
- 1 cup light-colored honey or sugar
- 2 tablespoons lemon juice
- ¼ teaspoon sea salt

1 Combine the strawberries, sugar, honey, lemon juice, and salt in a medium pot over medium heat. Using a handheld masher, break the strawberries into smaller pieces, leaving some larger chunks. Bring to a gentle boil and simmer for 5 minutes.

2 Divide the strawberry mixture evenly between two 18- by 13-inch rimmed baking pans. (I set up a table next to my car and ladle the mixture into the pans outside, so they don't have to travel far.) You can use smaller pans as well, as long as the mixture isn't deeper than ½ inch; otherwise it won't finish properly.

Recipe continues on next page

3 Now let the sun work its magic! Place the pans where they can receive 5 to 8 hours of direct sun but also be protected from insects. I position my car so that the dashboard is facing the sun and place a towel on the dash to protect it from spills. Using oven mitts, carefully place the pans on the dash. Use chopsticks or washcloths to shim the pans level if necessary, so that the jam cooks evenly.

4 Let the jam "cook," stirring every 1½ hours with a silicone spatula, until the jam is thick and has a glassy appearance, 5 to 8 hours. When you stir, make sure the strawberries around the edges and in the corners get mixed to the center as they will finish first, then spread the strawberries back into an even layer that fills the entire pan. To test the jam, drag a spatula through it; if it leaves a trail and doesn't immediately fill back in, it's done. The jam will thicken more once cool.

5 **To freeze:** Cool before freezing. Because it is thick, jam packs best in rigid containers.

NOTE: *You can also finish the jam in the oven if needed. Set the oven on its lowest temperature (use convection if you have it) and stir the jam every 20 minutes until finished. To spread the jam making over multiple days, make the recipe through step 2 and place the cooked strawberry mixture in the refrigerator for up to 3 days before jamming.*

Strawberries & Cream Baked Oatmeal

I love having a pan of baked oatmeal in the fridge to reheat for breakfasts and snacking. Sweet strawberries and creamy white chocolate are a splendid combination! This oatmeal is lightly sweetened, so feel free to serve it with a drizzle of maple syrup. If you don't have white chocolate, try milk or dark chocolate chips instead.

YIELD: 9 SERVINGS

    Cooking spray, for greasing pan

2 cups frozen whole strawberries

2 cups milk or nondairy alternative

⅓ cup sugar or honey

1 egg

2 teaspoons vanilla extract

¼ teaspoon sea salt

2 cups old-fashioned oats

⅓ cup white chocolate chips

1   Preheat the oven to 350°F (180°C). Grease a 9-inch square baking pan.

2   Place the strawberries on a cutting board and allow them to thaw for 10 minutes while you prepare the oatmeal.

3   Whisk together the milk, sugar, egg, vanilla, and salt in a large bowl. Stir in the oats.

4   Cut the partially thawed strawberries into quarters if they are large and into halves if they are small, then fold them into the oat mixture.

5   Pour the oat mixture into the prepared baking pan and use a spatula to push the oats down into the liquid, making sure they are all submerged. Sprinkle the top evenly with the chocolate chips.

6   Bake for 55 to 60 minutes, or until the edges are just starting to turn golden brown. Serve warm.

TIP: *Try this oatmeal with blueberries, raspberries, or blackberries!*

Beulah's Strawberry Salad

This is one of those famous "salads" from the upper Midwest that has absolutely no vegetables and probably no business being called a salad either, but it's a true delight! A staple at potlucks and picnics, this salad (okay, it's a gelatin dessert) has been served to me since I was little, courtesy of my Great-Aunt Beulah. This dish is presented in a decorative glass bowl with the main meal, not as a dessert, which is perhaps why it's allowed to be called a salad.

YIELD: 12 SERVINGS

    5 cups whole frozen strawberries, thawed

    1 cup thawed frozen or fresh mashed banana
      (about 3 medium whole)

    1 (8-ounce) can crushed pineapple (see Note)

    ⅓ cup roughly chopped walnuts

    ½ cup plus 1 tablespoon sugar

    3 tablespoons unflavored gelatin

    ⅛ teaspoon sea salt

    1 cup boiling water

    ⅔ cup sour cream

1 Place the strawberries in a large bowl and use a handheld masher to crush and break them up. Stir in the banana, the pineapple and all of its juice, and the walnuts.

2 Mix together the sugar, gelatin, and salt in a heatproof bowl. Add the boiling water and stir until the sugar dissolves.

3 Add the warm gelatin mixture to the fruit and stir until well combined.

4 Pour half of the mixture into an 8- to 10-cup glass bowl or pan. Refrigerate for 10 to 30 minutes, or until the gelatin is just starting to set on top. Let the remaining gelatin mixture stay at room temperature.

5 Spread the sour cream in an even layer on top of the gelatin, then spoon the remaining gelatin over the top.

6 Refrigerate until chilled and firm, at least 4 hours or overnight. Scoop with a spoon or cut into squares.

NOTE: *Do not use fresh pineapple, as the enzymes in it will prevent the gelatin from setting.*

SWEET POTATOES

If you're growing them yourself, make sure to cure sweet potatoes in a warm, humid environment after harvest to bring out their sweet taste. Just like regular potatoes, sweet potatoes need to be cooked or blanched before freezing to retain their quality. Any color sweet potato can be frozen.

Freezing Sweet Potato Mash

Mashed sweet potatoes can be reheated and topped with butter for a simple side dish, turned into sweet potato casserole, or used for cooking and baking—try the Whole-Wheat Sweet Potato Pancakes on page 169.

Prep. Peel the sweet potatoes and cut them into approximately 1-inch pieces. Steam until tender, about 20 minutes total, tossing them around at the 10-minute mark. Use a handheld masher to mash the sweet potatoes, or pulse them in a food processor until smooth.

Freeze. Sweet potato mash packs well in freezer bags or rigid containers. Consider freezing individual portions in a silicone muffin pan.

Heat. Thawed sweet potatoes can be heated in the microwave or on the stovetop in a covered pan with a splash of water.

Freezing Sweet Potato Cubes

Roasted sweet potato cubes can stand by themselves, and they also make a good base for combining with other veggies—serve them with roasted Brussels sprouts and onions, paired with black beans as a filling for tacos, or in a comforting soup with spicy sausage and kale.

Prep. Peel the sweet potatoes and cut into 1-inch cubes.

Roast. Toss the sweet potatoes with enough olive oil to lightly coat the pieces (about 1 tablespoon oil for every 4 cups sweet potatoes) on a large baking pan. Spread into a single layer, and roast in a 400°F (200°C) oven for 35 to 45 minutes, or until the sweet potato cubes are beginning to brown on the bottom.

Freeze. Cool before freezing. Cubed sweet potatoes pack best in freezer bags.

Heat. Sauté thawed sweet potato cubes in a small amount of oil until heated through, about 7 minutes. Alternatively, heat in a 350°F (180°C) oven for 10 minutes or in the microwave.

Smoky Roasted Sweet Potatoes

The spices and smoky paprika on these sweet potatoes go well with just about any meal—try them in quick dinners or easy breakfasts. My favorite way to serve them is with scrambled eggs and bacon.

YIELD: 6–8 SERVINGS

- 8 cups peeled and cut sweet potatoes, in 1-inch cubes (about 2½ pounds whole)
- 2 tablespoons extra-virgin olive oil, avocado oil, or melted lard
- 1 teaspoon sea salt
- 1 teaspoon granulated onion
- 1 teaspoon granulated garlic
- ½ teaspoon smoked paprika
- ¼ teaspoon dried thyme
- ⅛ teaspoon freshly ground black pepper

1 Preheat the oven to 400°F (200°C).

2 Pile the sweet potato cubes on a large baking pan, drizzle with the oil, then toss to coat. Evenly sprinkle the salt, onion, garlic, paprika, thyme, and pepper over the top, then toss again to coat.

3 Arrange the sweet potatoes in a single layer and bake for 35 to 45 minutes, or until tender and starting to brown on the bottom.

4 **To freeze:** Cool before freezing. Cubed sweet potatoes pack best in freezer bags.

5 **To heat:** Sauté thawed sweet potato cubes in a small amount of oil until heated through, about 7 minutes. Alternatively, heat in a 350°F (180°C) oven for 10 minutes or in the microwave.

Whole-Wheat Sweet Potato Pancakes

These pancakes are hearty with a somewhat custardy center, and the sweet potato gives them a natural sweetness. Whereas regular pancakes are a blank canvas for syrup and fruit sauces, these pancakes almost feel complete as they are (although a pat of butter and a drizzle of maple syrup doesn't hurt!). One of my favorite ways to eat them is folded in half like a taco with Swiss cheese and ham inside.

YIELD: 9 PANCAKES

- 1½ cups whole-wheat flour
- 2 teaspoons baking powder
- ¼ teaspoon ground cinnamon
- ⅛ teaspoon sea salt
- 1¼ cups milk or nondairy alternative
- 1 cup frozen sweet potato mash (page 167), thawed
- 2 eggs
- 1 tablespoon avocado oil or melted coconut oil
- 1 teaspoon vanilla extract
- Butter, avocado oil, or coconut oil, for cooking

1 Whisk together the flour, baking powder, cinnamon, and salt in a large bowl.

2 Whisk together the milk, sweet potato, eggs, oil, and vanilla in a bowl. Pour this mixture into the flour mixture, and stir until just combined.

3 Preheat a griddle or cast-iron pan over medium-low heat. Grease with butter. For each pancake, spoon ¼ cup batter on the griddle. Use the back of the spoon to spread out and flatten each pancake to about 5 inches in diameter.

4 Because these pancakes are dense, cooking at a lower temperature ensures they cook all the way through. Cook until the bottom is deep golden brown, 3 to 4 minutes. Flip and cook the second side for 3 to 4 minutes longer.

TOMATILLOS

Tomatillos are the plants that keep on giving in my garden. I planted them one time many years ago, and now volunteer tomatillos come up every year—it's fantastic! I prefer my tomatillos a little on the "green" side, so I pick them once they've completely filled their husks and are just starting to burst out of them.

Freezing Raw Tomatillos

Similar to tomatoes, tomatillos can be frozen raw if you're short on time or waiting for more to ripen. If you're able to process them into salsa or sauce before freezing, the finished product will be better, so only freeze them raw if it's necessary.

Prep. Remove the husks and rinse thoroughly, as tomatillos have a tacky surface that tends to attract dirt. Set the tomatillos on a towel to dry before freezing. Freeze whole or cut into halves or quarters, which will take up less freezer space.

Freeze. Tomatillos pack best in freezer bags.

Green Enchilada Sauce

This is a versatile sauce to have on hand in the freezer—it's smooth, full of robust flavor from the peppers and aromatics, and so much tastier than store-bought canned enchilada sauce. Using several types of peppers gives this sauce a well-rounded flavor, but feel free to substitute an additional green bell pepper if you don't have a poblano.

YIELD: ABOUT 6 CUPS

- 1 tablespoon extra-virgin olive oil, avocado oil, or lard
- ½ large yellow onion, diced
- 10 cups quartered tomatillos (about 3 pounds whole)
- 1½ cups water
- 1 large poblano pepper, diced
- 1 large green bell pepper, diced
- 2 jalapeños, cored, deseeded, and diced
- 4 garlic cloves, minced
- 1 teaspoon sea salt
- 1 teaspoon dried oregano
- ½ teaspoon ground cumin

1 Heat the oil in a large pot over medium-high heat. Add the onion and sauté, stirring occasionally, until tender, about 7 minutes.

2 Stir in the tomatillos, water, poblano, bell pepper, jalapeños, garlic, salt, oregano, and cumin. Simmer, uncovered, stirring occasionally, until the mixture has thickened and reduced, about 30 minutes.

3 Allow the tomatillo mixture to cool to a safe handling temperature, then use an immersion blender or transfer to a countertop blender and blend on high until smooth.

4 **To freeze:** Chill the enchilada sauce overnight in the refrigerator before freezing, so that the flavors can meld. Enchilada sauce packs well in freezer bags or rigid containers.

TOMATOES

Freezing tomatoes is truly the "choose your own adventure" game of the preserving world! They can be frozen raw in every form or transformed into any sauce, salsa, or condiment you can dream up.

Freezing Whole Raw Tomatoes

Freezing whole raw tomatoes is a handy time extender when you can't get to preserving them or don't have enough for a recipe. Throw them right into the freezer whole! Bonus: The skins peel off easily once thawed. The only downside is that they will lose some of their garden-fresh flavor. I freeze whole raw tomatoes for later use only if it's truly necessary.

Prep. Wash the tomatoes and remove the stems before freezing. If you want to prep your tomatoes one step further, core and cut them into large chunks before freezing. Cherry tomatoes can be frozen whole for throwing into sauce or processing later.

Freeze. Whole tomatoes pack best in freezer bags.

Special thawing instructions. The skins of frozen whole tomatoes will start to slip off as they thaw and will be easy to remove if desired. Frozen raw tomatoes will give off a significant amount of liquid when thawed, and this liquid contains loads of flavor. When thawing large quantities of tomatoes to process, there's a decision to

TYPES OF TOMATOES

Paste tomatoes are workhorses in my preserving kitchen. These medium-sized, usually elongated, flavorful tomatoes have a lot of body and not a lot of seeds. This makes them perfect for cooking down into sauce.

Beefsteak, globe, and "slicer" tomatoes are typically round and contain more gel and seeds than other varieties. While they can be cooked down into sauce, it takes a while, and you will get less sauce per pound of tomatoes than with paste tomatoes. Some beefsteak varieties are meatier than others and better suited to saucing.

Cherry and grape tomatoes are small tomatoes that come in many different shapes. They usually have a significant amount of gel and seeds inside.

be made: Preserve all that flavor by including the liquid, which will increase the time it takes to boil down the tomatoes, or discard the liquid and save time but compromise the flavor. The choice is yours. My advice is to keep it!

Freezing Diced Tomatoes

Tomatoes can be diced and frozen raw, which is handy for throwing into soups and stews. They can also be cooked and frozen, so they are similar to canned diced tomatoes.

Prep. For raw diced tomatoes, simply dice and freeze. For cooked diced tomatoes, paste varieties will work best.

Remove the skins (see page 176), then dice the tomatoes and place them in a large pot. Simmer, stirring occasionally, until the tomatoes are tender and some of the liquid has evaporated, 20 to 40 minutes depending on quantity.

Freeze. Cool cooked tomatoes before freezing. Diced tomatoes pack well in freezer bags or rigid containers.

Freezing Tomato Purée

One of the most versatile of all the tomato products, tomato purée can be used as the base for pasta or pizza sauce, simmered down into tomato paste or ketchup, or added to soups and chili. Use it wherever you need

tomato flavor. About 1 pound of paste tomatoes will yield 1 cup of finished purée.

Prep. Start with any quantity of paste tomatoes. Purée can also be made from meaty beefsteak or heirloom tomatoes, but the cooking time will be longer because of the higher water content. Core the tomatoes and cut them into large chunks.

Cook. Put the tomatoes into a large pot and simmer, uncovered, over medium heat, stirring frequently, until the tomatoes have become tender, 45 to 75 minutes depending on the quantity.

Allow the tomatoes to cool to a safe handling temperature, then run them through a food mill. Alternatively, use a blender to purée the tomatoes, then work them through a fine-mesh sieve to remove the seeds and skins.

Pour the purée back into the pot and bring it back to a simmer. Cook, stirring frequently, until the purée has thickened and is reduced by about one-quarter of its original volume. Cook longer for a thicker purée.

Freeze. Cool before freezing. Tomato purée packs well in freezer bags or rigid containers.

Freezing Oven "Sun-Dried" Tomatoes

Tomatoes that are oven-dried, or "half-dry," as I often call them, have some of their moisture removed, but they aren't completely dry and are not shelf-stable. I like that they have a little body to them, and they're my first choice for topping pizza or focaccia without making it soggy. Extremely versatile, these can be added to anything from quiche and beef stew to pasta salad.

The best tomatoes for oven-drying are small paste or meaty cherry varieties. My favorite variety for this is called Juliet, but many types will work.

Prep. Cut the tomatoes in half to expose the seeds, but don't remove them. Place the tomatoes cut-side up in a single layer on a parchment paper–lined baking pan.

Bake at 400°F (200°C) for 30 minutes, then reduce the heat to 350°F (180°C) and bake for 15 to 30 minutes longer, depending on the size of the tomatoes. They are finished when they're just turning brown on the bottom and appear dried out on the top.

Freeze. Flash freeze, then transfer to a freezer bag for storage. Oven-dried tomatoes pack well in freezer bags or rigid containers.

Veggie-Loaded Marinara Sauce

With an impressive diversity of vegetables, this sauce is practically a complete meal. We cook up a pound or two of ground beef or Italian sausage, pour in the sauce, and serve over pasta for an easy dinner . . . all while reminiscing about last season's harvest with every bite. I love that this sauce is a snapshot in time of what's growing in the summer garden. It's adaptable to whatever is in season, and as long as the veggies are fresh, you can't go wrong!

YIELD: ABOUT 12 CUPS

- 20 cups deseeded (see page 176) and roughly chopped tomatoes (about 10 pounds whole; see Note)
- 1 large onion, sliced
- 1 bell pepper, sliced
- 2 cups sliced zucchini
- 2 cups chopped green beans
- 1 large carrot, thinly sliced
- 5 garlic cloves, thinly sliced
- 2 teaspoons sea salt
- ¼ cup chopped fresh basil
- ¼ cup chopped fresh parsley

1 Place the tomatoes in a large pot over medium heat, cover, and simmer, stirring occasionally, until the tomatoes are tender, about 25 minutes.

2 Make a mental note of how high the tomatoes are in the pot. Continue cooking, uncovered, stirring occasionally, until the tomatoes have reduced by slightly more than half, about 2½ hours.

3 Allow the tomatoes to cool to a safe handling temperature, then use an immersion blender, or transfer to a countertop blender and blend on high until smooth. Work in batches if needed.

4 Return the puréed tomatoes to the pot and again make a mental note of how high the tomatoes are in the pot. Bring to a simmer over medium heat and cook, stirring occasionally, until the tomato purée is reduced by one-quarter and is thick like typical marinara sauce, about 1½ hours longer.

5 Stir in the onion, bell pepper, zucchini, green beans, carrot, garlic, and salt. Continue cooking, stirring occasionally, until the vegetables are tender, about 1 hour.

6 Remove from the heat and stir in the basil and parsley.

7 **To freeze:** Chill the marinara sauce overnight in the refrigerator before freezing, so that the flavors can meld. Marinara packs well in freezer bags or rigid containers.

8 **To heat:** Simply warm the sauce and serve.

NOTE: *Use paste tomatoes or a mix of paste and meaty beefsteak types and heirlooms. Using at least 60 percent paste tomatoes will give the best finished product. Cherry tomatoes won't work well here.*

HOW TO DESEED TOMATOES

Tomato skins have a lot of flavor, so anytime they can be puréed into the sauce, I do so. Tomato seeds are a different story, and I don't care for them in most recipes. Even my high-powered blender doesn't pulverize them reliably, so I often remove them before cooking.

Cherry tomatoes. Carefully pierce the bottom of the tomato with a paring knife or other small knife with a sharp point. This will control which direction the seeds come out, so they won't explode all over you and your kitchen. Squeeze the seeds and gel into a deep bowl.

Paste tomatoes. Small paste tomatoes can be deseeded following the same "poke and squeeze" method as cherry tomatoes. For large or especially thick paste tomatoes, I cut them in half through their middle (the short way, not top to bottom), then squeeze out the seeds from each half. A quick flick of the wrist helps remove the seeds from deep in the tomato.

Round, beefsteak, and heirloom tomatoes. The seeds in round tomatoes are best exposed by cutting the tomato in half along its equator. Hold the tomato half over a bowl and squeeze it gently while rotating it in your hand. A gentle touch is all you need—finesse in working out the seeds is better than completely squishing the tomato.

Using a food mill. If you prefer to process tomatoes with a food mill, many of the tomato recipes in this book can be adapted to this technique. A food mill crushes the cooked tomatoes by pushing them through a perforated disk, thereby separating the skins and seeds from the flesh and juice.

HOW TO PEEL PASTE TOMATOES

Make a small X in the bottom of each tomato. Place 3 to 5 tomatoes at a time into a large pot of boiling water and cook for 30 to 60 seconds, or until you start to see the skin pull away from the bottom where they were cut. Remove the tomatoes with a slotted spoon onto a baking pan. While the tomatoes are still warm, peel off the skins.

Italian-Inspired Marinara Sauce

This marinara won't taste like store-bought, and that's a *good* thing! With fresh tomatoes, garlic, and basil, it's reminiscent of a traditional sauce you'd find in the Italian countryside. Simple and tasting of juicy homegrown tomatoes, this sauce is glorious in any pasta dish.

YIELD: ABOUT 8 CUPS

3 tablespoons extra-virgin olive oil

⅓ cup thinly sliced garlic

16 cups deseeded (see opposite page), roughly chopped paste tomatoes (about 8 pounds whole)

1 teaspoon sea salt

1 teaspoon dried oregano

¼ teaspoon crushed red pepper

2 tablespoons finely chopped fresh basil

1 Heat the oil in a large pot over low heat, add the garlic, and cook until the garlic is fragrant and just starting to brown, 3 to 4 minutes. Quickly stir in the tomatoes to stop the garlic from cooking. Cover and increase the heat to medium. Simmer, stirring occasionally, until the tomatoes are tender, about 20 minutes.

2 Stir in the salt, oregano, and crushed red pepper.

3 Make a mental note of how high the tomatoes are in the pot. Continue cooking, uncovered, stirring occasionally, until the tomatoes have reduced by slightly more than half, about 2 hours.

4 Remove from the heat and stir in the basil.

5 Allow the tomato mixture to cool to a safe handling temperature, then use an immersion blender, or transfer to a countertop blender and blend on high until smooth.

6 **To freeze:** Chill the marinara sauce overnight in the refrigerator before freezing, so that the flavors can meld. Marinara packs well in freezer bags or rigid containers.

Garden Tomato Salsa

This classic salsa has plenty of big flavors from the fresh tomatoes, peppers, onions, and garlic. Puréed salsas freeze better than chunky ones, so giving this a whirl in the blender after cooking will ensure it comes out of the freezer just as good as it went in. Leave the seeds in one or two of the jalapeños if you like your salsa spicy.

YIELD: ABOUT 9 CUPS

10 cups peeled, deseeded (see opposite page), diced paste tomatoes (about 8 pounds whole)

2 large green bell peppers, diced

2 medium red onions, diced

4 jalapeños, cored, deseeded, and diced

6 garlic cloves, minced

⅓ cup lime juice

⅓ cup distilled white vinegar

⅓ cup tomato paste

2 teaspoons sea salt

2 teaspoons sugar (optional)

1 Place the tomatoes in a large pot along with the bell peppers, onions, jalapeños, garlic, lime juice, vinegar, tomato paste, salt, and sugar, if using. Bring to a boil, then simmer gently, stirring occasionally, until the sauce has reduced and thickened, about 1 hour.

2 Allow the salsa to cool to a safe handling temperature, then transfer to a countertop blender and blend gently until just lightly puréed, 5 to 10 seconds.

3 **To freeze:** Chill the salsa overnight in the refrigerator before freezing, so that the flavors can meld. Salsa packs well in freezer bags or rigid containers.

Roasted Cherry Tomato Pizza Sauce

While I was attending college, one of my favorite jobs was working for a local family-owned pizza shop as a cook and supervisor. We made fresh pizza sauce every day, and I'm sure I whipped up thousands of pizzas! I like my sauce to be thick and generously seasoned with garlic and Italian spices—like this one. Making pizza sauce is my favorite way to make use of the copious amounts of cherry tomatoes we grow every year.

12 cups deseeded (see page 176) cherry tomatoes (see Note)

2 tablespoons extra-virgin olive oil

3 tablespoons lemon juice

1 tablespoon chopped fresh garlic

1½ teaspoons sea salt

1 tablespoon dried oregano

2 teaspoons dried basil

2 teaspoons dried parsley

1 teaspoon granulated onion

1 teaspoon granulated garlic

½ teaspoon dried rosemary

¼ teaspoon crushed red pepper

1 Preheat the oven to 350°F (180°C).

2 Place the tomatoes on an 18- by 13-inch rimmed baking pan. You may divide the tomatoes between two smaller pans if needed. Drizzle the tomatoes with the oil and toss to coat. Bake for 90 minutes, rotating the pan once halfway through cooking.

3 Allow the tomatoes to cool to a safe handling temperature, then transfer to a countertop blender. Add the lemon juice, fresh garlic, salt, oregano, basil, parsley, onion, granulated garlic, rosemary, and crushed red pepper. Blend on high until smooth, about 30 seconds.

4 **To freeze:** Chill the pizza sauce overnight in the refrigerator before freezing, so that the flavors can meld. Because it is thick, pizza sauce packs best in rigid containers. I freeze pizza sauce in 1-cup portions, which is enough to sauce two 10-inch pizzas.

NOTE: *You can also use paste tomatoes or a combination of paste and cherry tomatoes. Deseed and chop paste tomatoes into 2-inch pieces before measuring.*

❄ FOR THE FREEZER

Tomato Bruschetta Topping

Eating homegrown tomatoes with garlic and basil in the off-season is a true pleasure. This chopped tomato mixture retains an impressive amount of freshness in the freezer. While the topping is traditionally served (and hard to beat!) on toasted bread, try it on scrambled eggs or chicken.

YIELD: 2 CUPS

2 tablespoons extra-virgin olive oil

2 teaspoons minced garlic

4 cups deseeded (see page 176) and diced paste or heirloom tomatoes (about 1½ pounds whole)

1 teaspoon white wine vinegar

½ teaspoon sea salt

2 tablespoons finely chopped fresh basil

1 Heat the oil in a skillet over low heat. Add the garlic and sauté until fragrant and just starting to brown, about 3 minutes.

2 Stir in the tomatoes, vinegar, salt, and basil, and gently simmer until the tomatoes are heated through, about 5 minutes.

3 **To freeze:** Cool before freezing. Bruschetta topping packs well in freezer bags or rigid containers.

❄ FOR THE FREEZER

Tikka Masala Simmer Sauce

Generously spiced and concentrated with homegrown tomato flavor, this sauce is a favorite to keep stashed in the freezer for when that craving for Indian food hits. You will use about 1 cup of finished sauce for 1½ pounds of chicken, or a similar quantity of a meat alternative, so freeze in whatever quantity you will need for an average-size dinner in your home.

YIELD: ABOUT 4 CUPS

FOR FREEZING

- 4 tablespoons butter or avocado oil
- ½ large yellow onion, diced
- 4 garlic cloves, minced
- 4 teaspoons garam masala
- 1 teaspoon ground ginger
- 1 teaspoon ground turmeric
- 1 teaspoon paprika
- 1 teaspoon sea salt
- 4 cups tomato purée (page 173)
- 2 teaspoons firmly packed brown sugar

FOR SERVING

- Heavy cream or coconut milk
- Chopped fresh cilantro (optional)

1 Melt the butter in a medium pot over medium heat, then sauté the onion until soft, about 7 minutes.

2 Add the garlic, garam masala, ginger, turmeric, paprika, and salt. Cook, stirring almost continuously, for 1 minute to toast the spices.

3 Stir in the tomato purée and sugar, and bring to a simmer. Cook, uncovered, stirring occasionally, until the sauce has thickened and is reduced by nearly half, about 30 minutes.

4 **To freeze:** Chill the tikka masala sauce overnight in the refrigerator before freezing, so that the flavors can meld. Because it is thick, tikka masala sauce packs best in rigid containers.

5 **To heat:** Add the sauce and cream to a large pan with the cooked protein. Use ⅓ to ½ cup of cream for every 1 cup of sauce. Simmer until the sauce is thick and coats the protein, about 7 minutes. Serve and garnish with cilantro, if using.

Heirloom Tomato Soup

The star of my garden, heirloom tomatoes have unique flavor characteristics you won't find in commercially grown or hybrid varieties. This tomato soup is a splendid way to showcase them! Using paste tomatoes along with the heirlooms makes a soup that is rich and complex and with good texture.

YIELD: ABOUT 8 CUPS

- 1 tablespoon extra-virgin olive oil
- ½ medium yellow onion, finely diced
- 1 tablespoon all-purpose flour or gluten-free flour blend
- 6 cups deseeded (see page 176) and diced heirloom tomatoes
- 6 cups deseeded (see page 176) and diced paste tomatoes
- 2 cups water
- 3 garlic cloves, minced
- 1 tablespoon fresh thyme
- 1 teaspoon sugar
- 1 teaspoon sea salt
- ¼ teaspoon freshly ground black pepper

1 Heat the oil in a large pot over medium heat. Add the onion and sauté until soft, about 7 minutes. Stir in the flour and cook for 2 minutes longer.

2 Add the tomatoes, water, garlic, thyme, sugar, salt, and pepper. Bring to a boil and simmer, uncovered, stirring occasionally, until reduced by one-third, about 60 minutes. Make sure to scrape the bottom of the pot while stirring, so that the tomatoes don't stick and burn.

3 Allow the soup to cool to a safe handling temperature, then use an immersion blender or transfer to a countertop blender and blend on high until smooth.

4 **To freeze:** Cool before freezing. Tomato soup packs well in freezer bags or rigid containers.

5 **To heat:** When thawed, this soup will appear separated (but still taste great). If you want a more homogeneous soup, purée on high in a blender to bring the ingredients back together. Heat in a saucepan on the stove or in the microwave.

WINTER SQUASH & PUMPKIN

All pumpkins are winter squashes, but not all winter squashes are pumpkins. Pumpkins are simply members of the squash family that are round, orange, and ribbed. While each different type of winter squash has its own characteristics, most orange-fleshed sweet types (think butternut, buttercup, kabocha, 'Candy Roaster', Hubbard) are interchangeable and can be used when a recipe calls for "pumpkin." Smaller, lighter-fleshed varieties (such as acorn, spaghetti, and delicata) are better suited for other preparations, mainly roasting or panfrying.

Freezing Winter Squash Purée

Squash purée is good for more than just pies! Top it with butter and a drizzle of maple syrup for a comforting side dish, cook it into oatmeal, or bake with it. Squash should be cooked before being frozen, and the best way to do that is roasting. This concentrates the flavor and ensures that your squash purée will be thick and not watery. Frozen winter squash purée can be used anywhere you would use canned pumpkin.

Prep. Use a vegetable brush or washcloth to scrub the outside of the squash. Using a sharp knife, carefully cut off the very top of the squash to remove the stem. Cut the squash in half from top to bottom, and use a spoon to scrape out the stringy guts and seeds.

Roast. Place the squash cut-side down on a rimmed baking pan, and roast in a 400°F (200°C) oven for 45 to 75 minutes, depending on size. The squash is done when it is soft, which you can feel by poking the rind. Allow the squash to cool to a safe handling temperature, then use a spoon to scoop out the flesh. Process the squash in a food processor or blender until smooth, about 30 seconds.

Freeze. Squash packs well in freezer bags or rigid containers. Consider freezing ½-cup portions in a silicone muffin pan.

Freezing Winter Squash Cubes

Squash cubes can be added to quiche and egg scrambles, tossed into soups and stews, and added to salads and pasta dishes. Try combining them with roasted root vegetables like carrots and rutabagas for a filling side dish or with fried apples for a breakfast hash. Use orange-fleshed squash like butternut and kabocha or lighter-colored squash like acorn and delicata here.

Prep. Use a vegetable brush or washcloth to scrub the outside of the squash. Use a vegetable peeler or sharp knife to remove the hard outer rind. Cut off the very top of the squash to remove the stem. Cut the squash in half from top to bottom, and use a spoon to scrape out the

Don't Toss the Seeds!

Seeds from *any* type of edible squash can be roasted into a tasty snack. Separate the seeds from the stringy flesh, then rinse them. Make a brine with 1 teaspoon sea salt and 2 cups water, and soak the seeds for 6 to 12 hours. Drain and pat them dry, then toss them with extra-virgin olive oil and any seasonings you'd like. Bake at 325°F (160°C) for 35 to 45 minutes, or until they turn golden.

stringy guts and seeds. Cut the squash into approximately 1-inch cubes.

Roast. Toss the squash with enough olive oil to lightly coat the pieces (about 1 tablespoon oil for every 5 cups squash) on a large baking pan. Roast in a 400°F (200°C) oven for about 40 minutes, or until the squash cubes are golden brown.

Freeze. Cool before freezing. Squash cubes pack best in freezer bags.

Savory Roasted Squash Cubes

Smaller squash with lighter-colored flesh and more tender skin, what I like to call "dinner squash" (think acorn and delicata), have a notoriously short storage life and are worth freezing if you have a lot of them. My favorite preserving method is to roast them with savory spices. Warm and serve this squash as a side dish, or add it to a hearty winter salad. Deeper orange-fleshed squash will also work with this recipe.

YIELD: 4 SERVINGS

- 5 cups peeled, cubed squash, in 1-inch pieces
- 1 tablespoon extra-virgin olive oil, avocado oil, or melted lard
- ½ teaspoon sea salt
- ½ teaspoon granulated garlic
- ½ teaspoon granulated onion
- ½ teaspoon ground sage
- ¼ teaspoon dried oregano
- ¼ teaspoon ground turmeric
- ⅛ teaspoon ground cinnamon

1 Preheat the oven to 400°F (200°C).

2 Pile the squash cubes on a large baking pan, drizzle with the oil, then toss to coat. Evenly sprinkle the salt, garlic, onion, sage, oregano, turmeric, and cinnamon over the top, then toss again to coat.

3 Arrange the squash in a single layer, and bake for about 40 minutes, or until just turning golden brown.

4 **To freeze:** Cool before freezing. Squash cubes pack best in freezer bags.

5 **To heat:** Sauté thawed sweet potato cubes in a small amount of oil until heated through, about 7 minutes. Alternatively, heat in a 350°F (180°C) oven for 10 minutes or in the microwave.

Creamy Butternut Squash Soup

This soup is like autumn in a bowl, and it stands firmly on the side of being savory, even though there's some sweetness from the apple, brown sugar, and cinnamon. This recipe calls for butternut squash, but any dark orange, flavorful winter squash will work well here. My favorite topper is pepitas (pumpkin seeds) that have been browned in butter, added right before serving.

YIELD: 4–6 SERVINGS

- 2 tablespoons butter, extra-virgin olive oil, or lard
- ½ medium yellow onion, diced
- 1 celery stalk, diced
- 2 garlic cloves, minced
- 1 apple, diced
- 4 cups vegetable broth
- 3 cups butternut squash purée (page 183)
- ¼ cup firmly packed brown sugar
- ½ teaspoon ground cinnamon
- ½ teaspoon ground ginger
- ¼ teaspoon freshly ground black pepper
- ¼ teaspoon ground turmeric
- Sea salt
- Heavy cream, coconut milk, broth, or water, for reheating
- Toasted pepitas (pumpkin seeds), croutons, crumbled bacon, or popcorn, for topping

1. Melt the butter in a large pot over medium heat. Add the onion and celery and sauté until soft, about 7 minutes. Stir in the garlic and apple, and cook for 5 minutes longer.

2. Add the broth, squash, sugar, cinnamon, ginger, pepper, and turmeric. Simmer, stirring occasionally until all the flavors are melded together, about 20 minutes.

3. Because some broths are saltier than others, taste the soup and add salt if necessary. I typically add about 1 teaspoon salt.

4. Allow the soup to cool to a safe handling temperature, then use an immersion blender, or transfer to a countertop blender and blend on high until smooth, about 30 seconds.

5. **To freeze:** Chill the soup overnight in the refrigerator before freezing, so that the flavors can meld. Squash soup packs best in rigid containers.

6. **To heat:** This soup goes into the freezer thick and should be thinned with a splash of cream, coconut milk, broth, or water before warming. Heat the soup on the stovetop or in the microwave. Finish with your topping of choice.

FOR THE TABLE

Squash Bolognese

A twist on an old favorite, this rich Bolognese uses puréed winter squash (pick your favorite type!) instead of tomatoes to make a flavorful sauce for tossing with pasta. It's incredibly comforting—the kind of meal well suited to a rainy or snowy day.

YIELD: 6–8 SERVINGS

- 2 tablespoons extra-virgin olive oil
- ½ pound lean ground beef
- ½ pound lean ground pork
- 1 medium yellow onion, finely diced
- 2 celery stalks, finely diced
- 2 cups water
- 2 cups frozen winter squash purée (page 183), thawed
- 2 garlic cloves, minced
- 2 tablespoons tomato paste
- 1½ teaspoons sea salt
- ½ teaspoon dried thyme
- ½ teaspoon dried oregano
- ¼ teaspoon freshly ground black pepper
- ¼ cup heavy cream
- ½ cup finely shredded Parmesan cheese
- 1 pound pasta

1 Heat 1 tablespoon of the oil in a skillet over medium heat. Add the beef and pork and cook, stirring and chopping the meat into small pieces, until browned, about 10 minutes. Drain any excess fat, and set the meat aside.

2 Heat the remaining 1 tablespoon oil in a large pot over medium heat. Add the onion and celery and sauté until tender, about 7 minutes.

3 Stir in the cooked meat along with the water, squash, garlic, tomato paste, salt, thyme, oregano, and black pepper. Simmer, uncovered, stirring occasionally, until the sauce is thick, about 45 minutes. Add up to an additional ½ cup water if the sauce gets too dry during cooking. Remove from the heat and stir in the cream and Parmesan.

4 While the sauce thickens, cook the pasta according to the directions on the package, then drain. Toss the sauce with the pasta and serve.

Pumpkin Bread with Cream Cheese Frosting

Soft and cakey with the flavors of fall, this bread is an old favorite family recipe. It's loaded with as much pumpkin and spice as I could stuff into one loaf! If you want to skip the frosting, try folding ½ cup of semisweet mini chocolate chips into the batter at the end for Chocolate Chip-Pumpkin Bread instead.

YIELD: ONE 9- BY 4-INCH LOAF

BREAD

    Cooking spray, for greasing pan

1½ cups frozen winter squash purée (page 183), thawed

¼ cup avocado oil or other neutral oil

¾ cup firmly packed brown sugar

3 eggs

1 teaspoon vanilla extract

1¼ cups all-purpose flour or gluten-free flour blend

2 teaspoons pumpkin pie spice

1 teaspoon ground cinnamon

1 teaspoon sea salt

1 teaspoon baking powder

½ teaspoon baking soda

FROSTING

3 ounces cream cheese, softened

3 tablespoons butter, softened

1 cup confectioners' sugar

½ teaspoon vanilla extract

1 To make the bread, preheat the oven to 350°F (180°C). Grease a 9- by 4-inch loaf pan and line the bottom with a rectangle of parchment paper (don't skip this step).

2 Place the squash, oil, brown sugar, eggs, and vanilla in a large bowl. Using a hand mixer or stand mixer fitted with a paddle attachment, beat together on high speed until combined, about 1 minute.

3 Stir together the flour, pumpkin pie spice, cinnamon, salt, baking powder, and baking soda in a bowl, then add it to the squash mixture and beat until just combined, about 15 seconds.

4 Pour the batter into the prepared loaf pan and smooth out the top with a silicone spatula.

5 Bake for 70 to 75 minutes, or until a toothpick inserted in the center comes out clean. Allow the bread to cool for 15 minutes in the pan, then remove it and place on a wire rack to finish cooling.

6 To make the frosting, combine the cream cheese and butter in a large bowl. Using a hand mixer or stand mixer fitted with a paddle attachment, beat together on high speed until combined, about 1 minute.

7 Add the confectioners' sugar and vanilla, and continue beating until well combined, about 1 minute. Cool the bread completely before spreading the frosting on the top of the loaf. Store in the refrigerator in an airtight container.

ZUCCHINI & OTHER SUMMER SQUASHES

Come late summer, we joke about sneaking bags full of zucchini into unlocked cars at the grocery store . . . but don't worry, it doesn't have to come to that! There are many creative ways to preserve a surplus of zucchini and other types of tender summer squash, such as yellow varieties and even pattypans.

Freezing Shredded Zucchini

Shredding is a handy way to use up large or overgrown zucchini. Shredded zucchini is versatile and can be added to just about anything you can dream up. Of course, there are classic baked goods such as zucchini bread, but shredded zucchini is also useful for adding extra veg to dishes like chili, meatloaf, eggs, oatmeal, blended soups, and even pancakes. You can apply this technique to other types of summer squash too.

Prep. Use a box grater or food processor with a shredding disc attachment to shred zucchini. If the zucchini is more than 2½ inches in diameter, cut it in half and scoop out the soft, spongy center before shredding. Shredded zucchini does not require blanching.

Freeze. Shredded zucchini packs well in freezer bags or rigid containers. Consider freezing ½-cup portions in a silicone muffin pan.

It's a good practice to measure shredded zucchini before freezing it and to write the amount on the freezer container. Once thawed, it will be difficult to accurately measure. If you have a favorite zucchini recipe, freeze shredded zucchini in the amount that it calls for to make baking easier.

Freezing Summer Squash Chunks

It seems like either you love frozen zucchini and other summer squash or you don't. I used to be in the latter camp until I figured out how to freeze these ingredients properly and which dishes they work best in. Hint: soup!

A hidden talent of frozen summer squash is adding bulk and nutrients to smoothies. Use chunks of frozen squash instead of ice cubes. When blended with bold flavors such as strawberries, blueberries, or chocolate, the squash all but disappears.

Prep. Use smaller, tender summer squash if the intention is to cook with it, and large, overgrown ones for smoothies. Cut squash in half lengthwise, then slice into 1-inch pieces. If the squash is more than 2½ inches in diameter, scoop out the soft, spongy center before slicing.

Blanch. Steam blanch (see page 10) for 4 minutes, tossing the squash around at the 2-minute mark. No ice bath is needed. Drain as much water as possible, then spread out the warm squash on a towel-lined pan to cool and dry.

Freeze. Squash chunks pack best in freezer bags. Consider flash freezing squash to use in smaller quantities.

COOKING & BAKING WITH FROZEN SHREDDED ZUCCHINI

Thawed zucchini will release a lot of liquid, which can affect how your recipe turns out. I wish there were a straightforward answer on how to deal with this issue. Whether or not to drain this extra liquid depends on what you're making, and finding the best approach might require trial and error.

Baked goods. I find that draining some of the liquid—up to half of it—works well for most baking recipes.

Soups and sauces. Liquid from thawed zucchini does contain nutrients, so in recipes where a little extra liquid won't hurt, I don't drain the zucchini before adding it.

Savory dishes. There are some instances where draining away all of the liquid is beneficial, as with meatballs, meatloaf, fritters, and quiche.

Freezing Zucchini Noodles, or "Zoodles"

Zoodles freeze perfectly, and I think they are better frozen-thawed than fresh! The process of blanching wilts and softens the zucchini, and once thawed, all they need is a quick sauté. Use zucchini noodles as a vegetable alternative to traditional pasta. Zucchini isn't the only summer squash you can make into noodles—try using yellow varieties too!

Prep. Making zoodles requires a gadget that will "noodle" them. There are different options available for this; the brand I use is called Spiralizer. A straight, medium-sized zucchini works best for turning into noodles.

Blanch. Steam blanch (see page 10) the zucchini noodles for 3 minutes, tossing them around at the 90-second mark. No ice bath is needed. Drain as much water from the zoodles as possible, then transfer to a towel-lined pan to dry.

Freeze. Zucchini noodles pack best in freezer bags.

Heat. Thaw zucchini noodles in the refrigerator overnight, then drain away any excess water. Heat a small amount of oil in a skillet over medium heat, add the zoodles, and sauté, stirring frequently until heated through, 2 to 3 minutes. Do not overcook.

Stewed Garlic Butter Zucchini

If you're looking for an easy way to pack a lot of zucchini into a little space, this is it! This zucchini is slow cooked in garlic butter until soft and tender, and it eats like mashed potatoes. We enjoy this as an easy side dish, although it's also great as the base for a pasta sauce or spread on a thick piece of toast. Because it's cooked until soft, the texture doesn't suffer after being frozen.

YIELD: ABOUT 3 CUPS

- 3 tablespoons butter or extra-virgin olive oil
- 8 cups 1-inch cubed zucchini or yellow summer squash (about 2½ pounds whole; see Note)
- ½ teaspoon sea salt
- 1 teaspoon minced fresh garlic

1 Melt the butter in a medium pot over low heat, then add the zucchini and salt. Cook, uncovered, stirring occasionally, until the zucchini is soft and easily smashed, about 45 minutes.

2 Stir in the garlic and cook for 5 minutes longer.

3 **To freeze:** Cool before freezing. Stewed zucchini packs best in rigid containers.

4 **To heat:** Place thawed zucchini in a covered pot with a splash of water and cook over low heat until heated through, about 7 minutes. It can also be heated in the microwave.

NOTE: *If the zucchini is more than 2½ inches in diameter, cut it in half and scoop out the soft, spongy center before cutting it into cubes.*

Herby Zucchini Pancakes

These tender and slightly crispy, savory pancakes are practically begging to be served with eggs for breakfast. And they're easy to reheat—just throw them in the toaster! If you're cooking for someone with a simpler palate, the fresh herbs can be omitted. Use traditional green zucchini or any variety of yellow summer squash.

YIELD: 6 PANCAKES

4	cups shredded zucchini or yellow summer squash (about 2 medium whole; see Note)
½	teaspoon sea salt, plus more for finishing
¼	cup all-purpose flour or gluten-free flour blend
1	tablespoon chopped fresh chives
1	tablespoon chopped fresh parsley
1	tablespoon chopped fresh basil
1	egg, beaten
2–3	tablespoons extra-virgin olive oil, avocado oil, or lard

1 Line a large bowl with a clean tea towel and place the shredded zucchini in it. Sprinkle the zucchini with salt and gently toss it around. Let the zucchini sit for 15 minutes.

2 Gather up the towel around the zucchini, forming it into a ball. Twist and tighten the top of the towel with one hand while using your other hand to squeeze the liquid out of the zucchini ball. Tighten and squeeze, tighten and squeeze, until you've released a little more than ½ cup of liquid and only a few drops still come out. Discard the liquid.

3 Return the zucchini to the bowl. Add the flour, chives, parsley, and basil. Mix until combined, then stir in the egg.

4 Heat 2 tablespoons of the oil in a skillet over medium-low heat. Drop the zucchini batter ¼ cup at a time into the pan, and use a fork to flatten it into a pancake about ¼ inch thick. Don't overcrowd the pan, and work in batches if needed. (When cooking in batches, you may need a little more oil for the pan for each subsequent round.)

5 Cook the pancakes until the bottoms are golden brown, about 7 minutes. Flip and cook for 5 minutes on the second side.

6 Transfer the pancakes to a paper towel-lined plate to drain. Sprinkle lightly with salt.

7 **To freeze:** Flash freeze the zucchini pancakes, then transfer to a freezer bag for storage.

8 **To heat:** Zucchini pancakes reheat best in the toaster, often needing two or three toaster cycles to heat all the way through from frozen.

NOTE: *If the zucchini is more than 2½ inches in diameter, cut it in half and scoop out the soft, spongy center before shredding.*

Index

EXPAND YOUR PRESERVING KNOW-HOW
with More Books from Storey

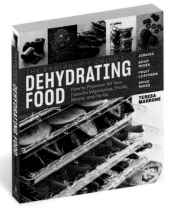

by Teresa Marrone

Stock your pantry with dried foods for year-round enjoyment. With step-by-step instructions, it's easy to use a tabletop dehydrator or the power of the sun to make apple rings, kale chips, fruit leather, baby food, and much more.

by Kirsten K. Shockey and Christopher Shockey

Even beginners can make their own fermented foods! This comprehensive guide offers more than 120 recipes for fermenting 64 different vegetables and herbs.

by Barbara Pleasant

This one-of-a-kind book shows you how to plan your garden so that you grow just the right amount of each crop to keep your pantry full of your favorites year-round.

JOIN THE CONVERSATION. Share your experience with this book, learn more about Storey Publishing's authors, and read original essays and book excerpts at storey.com. Look for our books wherever quality books are sold or call 800-441-5700.